THE ULTIMATE
TRUE BLOOD
TRIVIA GUIDE

SHERI R ANDERSON

To Jeff and Chloe.

CONTENTS

SEASON ONE
1.01 STRANGE LOVE
Written and Directed by Alan Ball

1. What song is heard playing on the young couple's radio as the first episode opens?
a. "Y'all'd Think She'd Be Good to Me."
b. "Bad Moon Rising."
c. "Strange Love."
d. "Som'thin' From Nuthin'."

2. What is the girl's name?
a. Kelly.
b. Tina.
c. Susie.
d. Lisa.

3. Name the convenience station in which the young couple encounters their first vampire.
a. Quik-E-Mart.
b. Super Save-A-Bunch.
c. Grabbit Kwik.
d. Grab-N-Go.

4. Who is seen interviewing Nan Flanagan on the store's television?
a. Jerry Springer.
b. Bill Maher.

c. Charlie Rose.

d. Larry King.

5. Nan Flanagan is the face of what organization?

a. American Vampire League.

b. Vampire Rights League.

c. Vampire Rights Association.

d. American Association of Vampires.

6. What nation perfected the production of synthetic blood, thereby allowing vampires to come "out of the coffin?"

a. China.

b. India.

c. United States.

 d. Japan.

7. Who sings the series' theme song, "Bad Things?"

a. Nathan Barr.

b. Jace Everett.

c. Lyle Lovett.

d. Dr. John.

8. Where does Maudette Pickens work?

a. Quik-E-Mart.

b. Super Save-A-Bunch.

c. Grabbit Kwik.

d. Merlotte's.

9. Which supernatural species is not represented in Season One?

a. Telepath.

b. Werewolf.

c. Shape shifter.

d. Vampire.

10. Where does Tara work prior to coming to Merlotte's?

a. Quik-E-Mart.

b. Super Save-A-Bunch.

c. Grabbit Kwik.

d. Grab-N-Go.

11. What does Tara read while on the clock at the above location?

a. *Last Scene Alive.*

b. *The Secret.*

c. *Shock Doctrine.*

d. *Grave Secret.*

12. Name Tara's manager.

a. Wayne.

b. Wyatt.

c. Wade.

d. Waylon.

13. What type of car does Tara drive?

a. Civic.

b. Gremlin.

c. Fury.

d. Nova.

14. What are the first names of the detested Rattrays?

a. Mack and Denise.

b. Matt and Debbie.

c. Mack and Debbie.

d. Matt and Denise.

15. Arlene's relationship with her children is established in episode one, when she is overheard discouraging them from what vice?

a. Painting each other with mustard.

b. Eating in bed.

c. Locking the babysitter in the bathroom.

d. Watching HBO.

16. Where did Jason read that everyone should have sex with a vampire at least once?

a. Playboy.

b. Penthouse.

c. Hustler.

d. Buns.

17. Name the vampire in Maudette's sex tape.

a. Malcolm.

b. Liam.

c. Charles.

d. Maxwell.

18. How long have vampires been "out of the coffin?"

a. One year.

b. A year and a half.

c. Two years.

d. Three years.

19. Prior to Bill Compton's arrival, when did Merlotte's last carry synthetic blood?

a. Six months earlier.

b. A year earlier.

c. A few months earlier.

d. Never.

20. How does Rattray describe Sookie to Bill?

a. Nutty as a fruitcake.

b. Mad as a hatter.

c. Screwy as a three dollar bill.

d. Crazy as a bedbug.

21. How old is Bill at the time he first enters Merlotte's?

a. 172.

b. 173.

c. 175.

d. 176.

22. How much does Mrs. Rattray think she can get per oz. of Bill's blood?

a. $200.

b. $300.

c. $400.

d. $500.

23. How many pints does she estimate she could drain from him?

a. 10-11.

b. 11-12.

c. 12-13.

d. 13-14.

24. In addition to the chain, what weapon does Sookie use to defend Bill and herself from the Rattrays?

a. A rock.

b. A gun.

c. A knife.

d. None. She used only the chain.

25 .What type of dog comes to check on Sookie after the Rattray encounter?

a. English shepherd.

b. Australian shepherd.

c. Terrier mix.

d. Labrador.

26. What trait does Sookie find most appealing in Bill?

a. He is a mystery.

b. She can't hear him.

c. His skin is cool.

d. He completes her.

27. Which of the following is not among the list of names Sookie expected Bill to have?

a. Basil.

b. Quentin.

c. Antoine.

d. Langford.

28. How does Sam describe most of his customers?

a. Stupid.

b. Lazy.

c. Cheap.

d. Drunk.

29. In what grade did Tara first mix drinks for her mother?

a. Kindergarten.

b. First.

c. Second.
d. Third.

30. In what grade did Sookie and Tara become best friends?
a. Kindergarten.
b. First.
c. Second.
d. Third.

31. What is Adele reading when Sookie returns home from her shift at Merlotte's?
a. Last Scene Alive.
b. The Secret.
c. Shock Doctrine.
d. Grave Secret.

32. Name Sookie's cat.
a. Josie.
b. Tina.
c. Dottie.
d. Lottie.

33. Who informs Jason of the Rattray encounter?
a. Rene.
b. Lafayette.
c. Hoyt.
d. Andy.

34. In a nod to the books, Jason's hat features what animal?
a. A panther.
b. A dog.
c. A wolf.
d. A tiger.

35. Name Jason's employer.
a. Renard Parish Road Crew.
b. Renard Parish Public Works.
c. Renard Parish Department of Transportation.
d. Renard Parish Department of Sanitation and Engineering.

36. Who informs Adele about Maudette's death?

a. Maxine Fortenberry.

b. Caroline Bellefleur.

c. Jane Bodehouse.

d. Everlee Mason.

37. Adele regularly attends meetings of what historical society?

a. Daughters of the Glorious Dead.

b. Decedents of the Glorious Dead.

c. Decendents of the Gracious Dead.

d. Daughters of the Gracious Dead.

38. Tara's name was inspired by *Gone with the Wind*. What specifically does she give as her mother's inspiration?

a. The heroine.

b. The movie.

c. The book.

d. The plantation.

39.Why does Sookie believe everyone in the bar is staring at her and Bill?

a. Because her brother is in trouble.

b. Because they are a bunch of nosey rednecks.

c. Because he is a vampire and she is mortal.

d. Because of her "ability."

40. What type of car does Sookie drive?

a. Civic.

b. Gremlin.

c. Fury.

d. Nova.

1.1 Answers

1. A. 2. A. 3. C. 4. B. 5. A. 6. D. 7 B. 8. C. 9. B. 10. B. 11. C. 12 D. 13. B. 14. A. 15. D. 16. C. 17. B. 18. C. 19. B. 20. D. 21. B. 22. D. 23. B. 24. C. 25. A. 26. B. 27. B. 28. A. 29. D. 30. A. 31. A. 32. B. 33. C. 34. A. 35. B. 36. D. 37. B. 38. D. 39. A. 40. A.

1.02 THE FIRST TASTE
Written by: Alan Ball
Directed by: Scott Winant

1. What is the source of Sookie's "first taste"?

a. Bill's neck.

b. Bill's right wrist.

c. Bill's left arm.

d. Bill's left hand.

2. In what appears to be a common occurrence, Tara comes home to find her mother passed out. What is playing on the television?

a. *The Bachelor.*

b. *America's Smartest Model.*

c. *Blind Date.*

d. *Singled Out.*

3. What is Tara's cereal of choice?

a. Lucky Charms.

b. Cap'n Crunch.

c. Frosted Flakes.

d. Trix.

4. To whom does Jason turn for comfort on the night following Maudette's death?

a. Sookie.

b. Tara.

c. Dawn.

d. Ray-Jean.

5. How long do Bud and Andy wait to show Jason Maudette's sex tape?

a. Two hours.

b. Six hours.

c. Twelve hours.

d. Fifteen hours.

6. Sookie awakens to find Bill licking her:

a. Wrist.

b. Neck.

c. Shoulder.

d. Head.

7. Flashback: Sookie's first dating memory ends in her dousing her date with:

a. Ketchup.

b. Mustard.

c. Mountain Dew.

d. Beer.

8. Flashback: Another date ends due to Sookie's date fantasizing about:

a. Jake Gyllenhaal in *Jarhead*.

b. Colin Farrel in *Tigerland*.

c. Zac Efron in *High School Musical*.

d. Vin Diesel in *The Fast and the Furious*.

9. Why does Sookie refuse to listen to the thoughts of her family?

a. It is personal.

b. It is private.

c. It is unethical.

d. It is too much information.

10. Meanwhile, at a party with her cousin Lafayette, Tara is approached by which would-be suitor?

a. Tareq.

b. Terrell.

c. Tyrone.

d. Tyrese.

11. To discourage the aforementioned suitor, Tara tells him that she is married to a:
a. Bounty hunter.
b. Hitman.
c. Mercenary.
d. Drug dealer.

12. Tara claims her fictitious husband once shot a man for buying her:
a. A CD.
b. A rum and coke.
c. A magazine.
d. A pack of cigarettes.

13. In what year was Bill Compton made vampire?
a. 1860.
b. 1865.
c. 1870.
d. 1875.

14. How old was he at the time?
a. 25.
b. 27.
c. 30.
d. 32.

15. After taking Bill's blood for the first time, Sookie claims to be more aware of the complexities of what food?
a. Sausage.
b. Eggs.
c. Bacon.
d. Cheese.

16. Sookie sarcastically states that all Jews have horns to draw attention to whose racial stereotyping?
a. Arlene's.
b. Andy's.
c. Tara's.
d. Maxine's.

17. Jason is often seen wearing a t-shirt for what band?
a. Marshall Tucker Band.
b. Lynyrd Skynyrd.
c. Kathleen Turner Overdrive.
d. Alabama Thunderpussy.

18. Bill masks the Rattrays' deaths by staging a tornado. Where does this occur?
a. Four Tracks Corners.
b. Bunkie.
c. Keatchie.
d. Monroe.

19. Bud Dearborn is skeptical of the Rattrays' cause of death, because tornados:
a. Travel.
b. Skip.
c. Hop.
d. Twist.

20. Who accompanies Bud to the Rattray home?
a. Mike Spencer.
b. Kenya Jones.
c. Kevin Ellis.
d. Andy Bellefleur.

21. What small morsel, found under a chair, offends Sookie's newly-sensitive sense of smell?
a. A cracker.
b. A cookie.
c. A tortilla chip.
d. A bread crust.

22. Adele makes the faux pas of offering what to Bill Compton upon his first visit?
a. Tea.
b. Coffee.
c. A sandwich.
d. A cookie.

23. Bill's mother was a member of what family?
a. Bellefleur.
b. Loudermilk.
c. Du Rone.
d. Bodehouse.

24. The Compton line ended with which of Bill's decendents?
a. Josiah.
b. Jesse.
c. Joshua.
d. Jonas.

25. What amendment does Bill expect to pass, granting equal rights to vampires?
a. EVA.
b. ERA.
c. ERV.
d. VRA.

26. Bill claims to have a clear memory of which Stackhouse ancestor?
a. Josiah.
b. Jesse.
c. Joshua.
d. Jonas.

27. How many slaves did Bill's family own?
a. One.
b. Two.
c. Three.
d. Four.

28. What was the name of the Compton's yard slave?
a. Minas.
b. Jonas.
c. Able.
d. Moses.

29. Which of the following is not an effect of Bill's blood in Sookie's system?
a. Keener senses.

b. Resistance to pain.

c. More active libido.

d. Ability to be found.

30. What is the common name for vampire hypnosis?

a. Glamouring.

b. Charming.

c. Alluring.

d. Entrancing.

31. Flashback: Young Sookie is able to prove her telepathy by picking what combination from the mind of her interrogator?

a. The color blue and the number three.

b. The color red and the number three.

c. The color blue and the number nine.

d. The color red and the number nine.

32. As what is her telepathy misdiagnosed?

a. ADD.

b. OCD.

c. Autism.

d. Turrets.

33. How old was Sookie when her parents were killed?

a. Five.

b. Six.

c. Seven.

d. Eight.

34. Sookie questions Bill on his skills as a vampire. Which of the following is not among those discussed?

a. Ability to read minds.

b. Ability to levitate.

c. Ability to turn invisible.

d. Ability to turn into a bat.

35. What is Dawn's apartment number?

a. 5042.

b. 5043.

c. 5044.

d. 5045.

36. Name Jane Bodehouse's drink of choice.

a. Gimlet.

b. Tom Collins.

c. Stinger.

d. Rum and coke.

37. Who comes to Sookie's defense when a customer grabs her backside?

a. Hoyt.

b. Sam.

c. Rene.

d. Terry.

38. Which of the following is not a member of the Steve Newlin's immediate family?

a. Theodore.

b. Lesley.

c. Yvette.

d. Bethany.

39. What is on the license plate of the strange car parked in Bill Compton's driveway?

a. Undead 1.

b. Fangs 1.

c. Blood 1.

d. Dead 1.

40. Bill's guests also have a bumper sticker bearing what slogan?

a. Honk if you're a fangbanger.

b. Honk if you're a blood donor.

c. I brake for O-.

d. I brake for A-.

1.2 Answers

   1. B. 2. B. 3. A. 4. C. 5. C. 6. D. 7. B. 8. A. 9. C. 10. B. 11. C. 12. A. 13. B. 14. C. 15. A. 16. C. 17. D. 18. A. 19. C. 20. A. 21. A. 22. C. 23. B. 24. B. 25.

D. 26. D. 27. C. 28. A. 29. B. 30. A. 31. D. 32. A. 33. D. 34. A. 35. C. 36. C. 37. C. 38. B. 39. B. 40. B.

1.03 MINE
Written by: Alan Ball
Directed by: John Dahl

1. Two of Bill's three vampire guests are named Diane and Malcolm. Name the third.

a. Jerry.

b. Liam.

c. Marcus.

d. Jack.

2. What does Diane do as Sookie enters the house?

a. Smells her hair.

b. Strokes her back.

c. Licks her face.

d. Kisses her cheek.

3. What, in Diane's opinion, is the best tasting blood there is?

a. Virgin.

b. Baby.

c. Christian.

d. Fairy.

4. What does Malcolm call Bill, upon meeting Sookie for the first time?

a. A poser.

b. A fraud.

c. A mainstreamer.

d. A fake.

5. What does Diane have tattooed on her arm?

a. Jerry.

b. Liam.

c. Marcus.

d. Jack.

6. Name the fangbanger accompanying Malcolm.

a. Jerry.

b. Liam.

c. Marcus.

d. Jack.

7. With what strain of Hepatitis is he infected?

a. A.

b. B.

c. C.

d. D.

8. He is trying to infect the vampires because they killed____.

a. Jerry.

b. Liam.

c. Marcus.

d. Jack.

9. When was Diane made vampire?

a. 1920s.

b. 1930s.

c. 1940s.

d. 1950s.

10. Bill refers to nest-sharing vampires as _____ unto themselves.

a. Laws.

b. Institutions.

c. Authorities.

d. Sovereignties.

11. According to Tara, Bill looks like he just stepped out of a movie about____.

a. Gettysburg.

b. A plantation.

c. A ghost town.

d. The Alamo.

12. Tara likewise claims that Sookie has always been _____ around men.

a. Awkward.

b. Jumpy.

c. Peculiar.

d. Crazy.

13. What does Bill offer as a possible explanation for Sookie's inability to hear his thoughts?

a. Lack of brainwaves.

b. Inhuman thought patterns.

c. Interspatial differences.

d. Lack of neural impulses.

14. To what does Bill attribute his ability to function?

a. The supernatural.

b. Sorcery.

c. Dark forces.

d. Magic.

15. Why doesn't Tara's mother think she needs to attend AA?

a. She's got Tara.

b. She's got a demon.

c. She's got Jesus.

d. She's got a plan.

16. What personal question does Tara ask Sam?

a. Are you happy?

b. Are you lonely?

c. Are you complete?

d. Are you in love?

17. Which of the following is not a strength Tara attributes to Sam?

a. He's hot.

b. He has a job.

c. He's not a vampire.
d. He's not a serial killer.

18. How long has it been since Tara last had sex?
a. Five months, two weeks.
b. Six months, three weeks.
c. Seven months, two weeks.
d. Eight months, three weeks.

19. When Sam offers Tara another drink, she says she will need at least _____ more.
a. Two.
b. Three.
c. Four.
d. Five.

20. Whose music can be heard in the background when Tara and Sam have sex for the first time?
a. Nathan Barr.
b. Allen Toussaint.
c. CC Adcock.
d. Jace Everett.

21. What unique item does Jason wear while having sex with Dawn?
a. Gloves.
b. Boots.
c. A cowboy hat.
d. A gag.

22. Despite Dawn holding a gun on him, Jason takes the time to _____ after sex.
a. Brush his hair.
b. Brush his teeth.
c. Floss.
d. Put on deodorant.

23. Dawn claims Jason is dumber than a box of what?
a. Toenails.
b. Hair.

c. Hammers.

d. Bricks.

24. What is playing on television when Jason returns home from Dawn's?

a. *Son of Dracula.*

b. *Blood of Dracula.*

c. *Countess Dracula.*

d. *House of Dracula.*

25. In a dream, Sookie goes to Bill's house for a late-night seduction. In the process, she interrupts Bill engaged in what activity?

a. Playing Wii.

b. Reading.

c. Playing the piano.

d. Watching tv.

26. What is embroidered on Sookie's pillowcase?

a. A heart.

b. A flower.

c. A star.

d. A bird.

27. Tara sneaks out after Sam _____ in his sleeps.

a. Barks.

b. Groans.

c. Growls.

d. Howls.

28. When she arrives at home, Tara's mother first hits her _____, then a bottle.

a. A lamp.

b. A book.

c. A vase.

d. A bowl.

29. What is written on the coffin in the Monroe vampires' nest?

a. Gott ist ein Vampir.

b. Gott ist der Teufel.

c. Gott ist der Tot.

d. Gott ist Tot.

30. Name the dead woman hanging in the nest.

a. Janella.

b. Janette.

c. Janet.

d. Janelle.

31. At what time of the morning does Adele find Sookie mowing the yard?

a. 8:00am.

b. 8:30am.

c. 9:00am.

d. 9:30am.

32. In spite of the early hour, it is already a sweltering _____.

a. 80 degrees.

b. 85 degrees.

c. 90 degrees.

d. 95 degrees.

33. Which of the following does Lafayette not offer Tara after her run-in with her mother?

a. Alcohol.

b. V.

c. Vicodin.

d. Ganja.

34. Lafayette's john offers Tara what pseudonym?

a. Dirk.

b. Randy.

c. Duke.

d. Rocky.

35. What is the john's profession?

a. Mayor.

b. Governor.

c. State Representative.

d. State Senator.

36. Sam is upset when he reads that a Starbucks is coming to _____.
a. Marthaville.
b. Bunkie.
c. Monroe.
d. Bon Temps.

37. Which of the following adjectives does Adele not use when explaining Bill's potential as a suitor?
a. Kind.
b. Smart.
c. Handsome.
d. Polite.

38. Name Sookie's grandfather.
a. Earl.
b. Edgar.
c. Edmond.
d. Edward.

39. Name Sookie's great uncle, who killed himself with a shotgun.
a. Fred.
b. Frank.
c. Francis.
d. Fritz.

40. To pay for V, Lafayette makes Jason dance around wearing a mask bearing whose likeness?
a. George Bush.
b. George W. Bush.
c. Barbara Bush.
d. Laura Bush.

1.3 Answers

1. B. 2. C. 3. B. 4. A. 5. D. 6. A. 7. D. 8. C. 9. B. 10. A. 11. B. 12. C. 13. A. 14. D. 15. C. 16. B. 17. C. 18. D. 19. B. 20. B. 21. A. 22. C. 23. B. 24. D. 25. B. 26. B. 27. A. 28. B. 29. D. 30. A. 31. C. 32. A. 33. B. 34. C. 35. D. 36. A. 37. A. 38. A. 39. C. 40. D.

1.04 ESCAPE FROM DRAGON HOUSE
Written by: Brian Buckner
Directed by: Michael Lehmann

1. Name the neighbor who overhears Jason's fight with Dawn.
a. Faye Lebvre.
b. Faye DuChien.
c. Faye LeFauve.
d. Faye DeBure.

2. How old was Dawn at the time of her death?
a. 20.
b. 21.
c. 22.
d. 23.

3. Who found Dawn's body?
a. Sam.
b. Sookie.
c. Jason.
d. Her neighbor.

4. Did the person listed above alter the crime scene in any way?
a. Yes. They cleaned up their own bloody footprints.
b. Yes. They covered victim's body.
c. Yes. They removed the sheet to smell it.
d. No. The crime scene was not altered.

5. While investigating the crime scene, Bud writes what in his notepad?
a. Killer had key.
b. Killer knew victim.
c. Killer wore gloves.
d. Killer in area.

6. Arlene lives in the same complex. What is her apartment number?
a. 5050.
b. 5049.
c. 5048.
d. 5047.

7. Who among the following was not waiting for news outside Dawn's apartment?
a. Maxine.
b. Hoyt.
c. Rene.
d. Sam.

8. Afraid of being caught, Jason consumes an entire vial of V. Where and when did he take it?
a. In Dawn's bathroom, as the cops arrived.
b. In the cop car, before leaving Dawn's.
c. In the cop car, en route to the police station.
d. At the police station, while waiting to be interrogated.

9. What maternal action does Maxine perform while waiting outside Dawn's?
a. She wipes Hoyt's nose.
b. She threatens to wash Hoyt's mouth out with soap.
c. She applies Hoyt's sunscreen.
d. She covers Hoyt's ears.

10. Who is Dawn's landlord?
a. Sam.
b. Maxine.
c. Andy.
d. Mike.

11. Neil Jones is Mike Spencer's new apprentice. Where is he from?
a. Georgia.
b. Kentucky.
c. Tennessee.
d. Alabama.

12. What is the most noticeable side-effect of Jason's V ingestion?
a. Paraphimosis.
b. Phimosis.
c. Priapism.
d. Peyronie's.

13. Bud believes that Jason is innocent based upon the fact he doesn't have what?
a. The brains.
b. A motive.
c. The sense God gave a pissant.
d. Fangs.

14. Who first mentions the fact that Jason was not read his Miranda rights?
a. Tara.
b. Bud.
c. Andy.
d. Jason.

15. According to Tara, school is just for white people looking for other white people_____.
a. To tell them they're right.
b. To read to them.
c. To teach them to hate black people.
d. To make them feel better about themselves.

16. Sookie overhears Hoyt thinking that Dawn's voice sounded like angels and _____.
a. Parakeets.
b. Hummingbirds.
c. Bluebirds.
d. Doves.

17. Jason reveals to Lafayette that he has been experiencing the negative effects of V since¬:
a. 9:00am.
b. 11:00am.
c. 1:00pm.
d. 3:00pm.

18. Jason likens his condition to:
a. Paralysis.
b. Gout.
c. Cancer.
d. Mumps.

19. What is Bill's preferred blood type?
a. O-.
b. A-.
c. AB-.
d. B+.

20. What, according to Bill, used to be the highest form of humor?
a. Flattery.
b. Riddles.
c. Puns.
d. Sarcasm.

21. What animal is depicted in the painting in Sam's office?
a. Snake.
b. Cat.
c. Dog.
d. Horse.

22. What make of car does Bill drive?
a. Lexus.
b. Mercedes.
c. Audi.
d. BMW.

23. Who finds Jason hiding in Merlotte's freezer?
a. Sookie.

b. Tara.

c. Sam.

d. Lafayette.

24. What does Jason use to hide the side-effects of his V ingestion?

a. A porterhouse.

b. A rib eye.

c. A t-bone.

d. A filet mignon.

25. Who appears with Sam in the picture behind the bar?

a. Maudette.

b. Dawn.

c. Sookie.

d. Arlene.

26. How old is Sookie?

a. 23.

b. 24.

c. 25.

d. 26.

27. Name the bartender at Fangtasia.

a. Long Shadow.

b. Black Eagle.

c. Hot Rain.

d. Dark Cloud.

28. What is Sookie's drink of choice?

a. Rum and coke.

b. Gin and tonic.

c. Vodka and tonic.

d. Tom Collins.

29. Name the vampire feeding in the Fangtasia bathroom at the time of the raid.

a. Tonya.

b. Taryn.

c. Torie.

d. Talia.

30. Which Fangtasia employee claims an inability to tell human ages?

a. Pam.

b. Eric.

c. Ginger.

d. Yvette.

31. Upon reading their minds, Sookie realizes that all anyone thinks about in Fangtasia is:

a. Sex.

b. Blood.

c. Death.

d. Eric.

32. Pam refers to her memory as:

a. A steel trap.

b. A vault.

c. A sponge.

d. A vice.

33. How late are the cops by the time Sookie finds out about the raid?

a. Five minutes.

b. Ten minutes.

c. Fifteen minutes.

d. Twenty minutes.

34. In what language is the music Bill plays on the way home from Fangtasia?

a. Cambodian.

b. Vietnamese.

c. Laotian.

d. Thai.

35. Bill and Sookie are pulled over by:

a. A federal marshal.

b. Shreveport PD.

c. Reston PD.

d. A state trooper.

36. Bill is offended that the officer calls him:
a. Bub.
b. Boy.
c. Kid.
d. Son.

37. Where does Bill suggest the cop check Sookie for evidence of feeding?
a. Carotid.
b. Femoral.
c. Thoracic.
d. Jugular.

38. Bill allows the officer to live, but takes his _____ as a souvenir.
a. Hat.
b. Badge.
c. Pants.
d. Gun.

39. While driving him home, Tara remembers Jason protecting her from:
a. Her teacher.
b. Sookie.
c. Her mother.
d. Child services.

40. Who is seen in Dawn's apartment as the episode ends?
a. Rene.
b. Sam.
c. Jason.
d. Andy.

1.4 Answers

1. A. 2. D. 3. B. 4. B. 5. A. 6. C. 7. D. 8. B. 9. C. 10. A. 11. B. 12. C. 13. D. 14. A. 15. B. 16. A. 17. D. 18. B. 19. A. 20. C. 21. C. 22. D. 23. B. 24. B. 25. B. 26. C. 27. A. 28. B. 29. B. 30. A. 31. A. 32. B. 33. C. 34. A. 35. D. 36. D. 37. B. 38. D. 39. C. 40. B.

1.05 SPARKS FLY OUT
Written by: Alexander Woo
Directed by: Dan Minahan

1. Unappreciative of the art of Tuvan throat singing, Sookie refers to it as what?
a. Howling.
b. Gargling.
c. Yodeling.
d. Grunting.

2. Sookie believes that, had she not been present, Bill would have tossed the cop aside like an old _____ bone.
a. Chicken.
b. Ham.
c. Dog.
d. T-.

3. Tara goes to Lafayette's to confront him about Jason's drug use. At what time does she arrive?
a. 2:00am.
b. 2:30am.
c. 3:00am.
d. 3:30am.

4. Tara compares giving drugs to Jason to giving _____ to a diabetic.
a. Hohos.
b. Twinkies.

c. Little Debbie's.

d. Oreos.

5. Lafayette was All-Parish in high school. What sport?

a. Basketball.

b. Football.

c. Baseball.

d. Track.

6. Gran tells Sookie the chance to know somebody who experienced the world differently would be:

a. A gift.

b. A blessing.

c. A miracle.

d. A challenge.

7. Tara has had a crush on Jason since she was:

a. Seven.

b. Eight.

c. Nine.

d. Ten.

8. According to Lafayette, blood is the only difference between a vampire and what?

a. A boudan sausage.

b. A vegetable.

c. A banana.

d. An oak tree.

9. Lafayette goes on to tell Jason that the blood of a new vampire is:

a. Strong.

b. Wild.

c. Unpredictable.

d. Dangerous.

10. Arlene describes Fangtasia patrons as freaks and people from where?

a. Georgia.

b. Arkansas.

c. Texas.

d. Alabama.

11. Andy becomes aware of Sookie's "gift" when she overhears him thinking about:

a. Her.

b. Tara.

c. Bill.

d. Maudette.

12. To what does Sookie compare Andy's thoughts?

a. Mice in a cage.

b. A dead-end street.

c. Bumper cars.

d. A burned out lightbulb.

13. Who tells Tara that Sam is taking Sookie to the DGD meeting?

a. Andy.

b. Arlene.

c. Sam.

d. Lafayette.

14. Prior to the start of the meeting, Maxine tries to cover a crucifix out of fear Bill will shrivel up like:

a. A raisin in the sun.

b. A salted slug.

c. Everlee Mason's neck.

d. Fat-back bacon.

15. Adele refers to Arlene's kids as:

a. Teacups.

b. Doodlebugs.

c. Munchkins.

d. Cutie pies.

16. What does the mayor's wife bring to the meeting?

a. Tuna cheese casserole.

b. Lemon meringue pie.

c. Ambrosia.

d. A jello mould.

17. How does Adele refer to the Civil War?

a. The War Between the States.

b. The War for Southern Independence.

c. The War of Attrition.

d. The Northern Invasion.

18. What is Bill's middle name?

a. James.

b. Edward.

c. Augustus.

d. Thomas.

19. Bill removes the American flag from a cross, stating that he wouldn't dream of putting himself before:

a. Old Glory.

b. The Stars and Stripes.

c. The Red, White and Blue.

d. This great nation.

20. Bill was a member of the _____Louisiana Infantry.

a. 23rd.

b. 28th.

c. 13th.

d. 17th.

21. In what year was the above infantry formed?

a. 1861.

b. 1862.

c. 1863.

d. 1864.

22. Where was it formed?

a. Monroe.

b. Bunkie.

c. Shreveport.

d. Marthaville.

23. The infantry was led by Col. Henry _____.

a. Gray.

b. Johnson.

c. Everett.

d. Mott.

24. How many Iraqis did Terry kill in Fallujah?

a. 15.

b. 18.

c. 20.

d. 23.

25. What does Royce bring to the meeting to annoy Bill?

a. Silver.

b. Garlic.

c. A crucifix.

d. Holy water.

26. Bill relates the story of the death of Toliver _____.

a. Harrison.

b. Hardwick.

c. Hardison.

d. Humphries.

27. Who presents Bill with a tintype of his family?

a. Mayor Norris.

b. Toliver's grandson.

c. Sid Matt Lancaster.

d. Reverend White.

28. Who asks to take a picture with Bill?

a. Everlee.

b. Maxine.

c. Rosie.

d. Arlene.

29. Following the meeting, whose curiosity leads him to order a Tru:Blood at Merlotte's?

a. Jason.

b. Rene.

c. Hoyt.

d. Royce.

30. What do his companions order?

a. Dixie.

b. Abita.

c. Heiner Brau.

d. Coors Light.

31. Who returns his/her burger because it might have AIDS?

a. Maxine.

b. Royce.

c. JB.

d. Coralee.

32. After confronting the person in question, Lafayette receives a high five from:

a. Jason.

b. Rene.

c. Hoyt.

d. Royce.

33. What does Sam drive?

a. Chevy Suburban.

b. Ford Bronco.

c. Jeep Wrangler.

d. Toyota Rav4.

34. Who, while celebrating her divorce, attracts Hoyt's attention?

a. Ricky Jean.

b. Billie Mae.

c. Donna Rae.

d. Randy Sue.

35. What does Bill offer Bud and Andy to drink when they come to his house for questioning?

a. Fanta.

b. Fresca.

c. RC.

d. Mountain Dew.

36. When he sees Andy admiring a tool by the fireplace, Bill tells him it is a:

a. Rotisserie.

b. Skewer.

c. Sandwich press.

d. Toaster.

37. Flashback: Lorena claims her husband was a member of the _____ Infantry.

a. 23rd.

b. 28th.

c. 13th.

d. 17th.

38. When he encounters Lorena, Bill is only 20 miles from home. In what direction?

a. Northeast.

b. Northwest.

c. Southeast.

d. Southwest.

39. How many children did Bill have?

a. One.

b. Two.

c. Three.

d. Four.

40. What was his rank in the Army?

a. Colonial.

b. Sargeant.

c. Major.

d. Lieutenant.

1.5 Answers

1. B. 2. A. 3. C. 4. A. 5. C. 6. B. 7. B. 8. A. 9. B. 10. B. 11. B. 12. A. 13. B. 14. D. 15. C. 16. C. 17. B. 18. D. 19. A. 20. B. 21. B. 22. A. 23. A. 24. C. 25. B. 26.

D. 27. A. 28. B. 29. C. 30. A. 31. B. 32. A. 33. B. 34. D. 35. B. 36. D. 37. C. 38. B. 39. B. 40. D.

1.06 COLD GROUND
Written by: Raelle Tucker
Directed by: Nick Gomez

1. Who was the first to arrive at Sookie's house after Gran's death?
a. Bill.
b. Sam.
c. Andy.
d. Bud.

2. Who brings Sookie a blanket?
a. Bill.
b. Sam.
c. Andy.
d. Bud.

3. Who tells Sam it is not the time to mark his territory?
a. Bill.
b. Mike.
c. Andy.
d. Bud.

4. Who determines Adele put up a fight, based upon the cuts on her hands?
a. Neil.
b. Mike.
c. Andy.
d. Bud.

5. Bill claims he came to Sookie's when he heard:
a. A scream.
b. A door.
c. A car.
d. A fight.

6. It is immediately questioned how he could hear it from:
a. Across the cemetery.
b. Down the street.
c. Across town.
d. Across the field.

7. Where did Sookie previously meet Neil?
a. Merlotte's.
b. Fangtasia.
c. The DGD meeting.
d. The Rattray crime scene.

8. What is the first thing Sookie does when everyone leaves?
a. Cleans.
b. Bathes.
c. Sleeps.
d. Screams.

9. What does Maxine bring Sookie the next day?
a. Tuna cheese casserole.
b. Lemon meringue pie.
c. Ambrosia.
d. A jello mould.

10. Sookie overhears Maxine thinking that she should have brought _____ instead.

a. German chocolate cake.
b. Peach cobbler.
c. Red velvet cake.
d. Peanut butter pie.

11. What kind of pie is "Gran's pie?"
a. Apple.

b. Cherry.

c. Pecan.

d. Pumpkin.

12. Who makes the mistake of touching it?

a. Maxine.

b. Tara.

c. Arlene.

d. Lafayette.

13. Tara advises Sookie to stop being:

a. Careful.

b. Dignified.

c. Normal.

d. Appropriate.

14. Sookie hasn't heard from Hadley in over:

a. Six months.

b. A year.

c. A year and a half.

d. Two years.

15. Who does Jason first hit upon learning of Adele's death?

a. Sookie.

b. Andy.

c. Hoyt.

d. Lafayette.

16. Lafayette is fascinated by white people's obsession with what?

a. Banana Pudding.

b. Jello.

c. Casserole.

d. Mayonaise.

17. Lafayette advises Tara to throw out the bad _____ cooking.

a. Mojo.

b. Juju.

c. Hoodoo.

d. Voodoo.

18. Sookie's nightmare wakes Bill during the daylight. What time is it?
a. 5:49.
b. 5:26.
c. 5:37.
d. 5:19.

19. Who describes Sookie's state as "dead to the world?"
a. Bill
b. Tara.
c. Sam.
d. Lafayette.

20. What song is playing as Bill stands guard outside Sookie's home?
a. "Lullaby."
b. "Half of You."
c. "Take Me Home."
d. "We'll Meet Along the Way."

21. Where is Adele buried?
a. Bon Temps Cemetery.
b. Sweet Home Cemetery.
c. Down Home Cemetery.
d. Amazing Grace Cemetery.

22. Who is the only character openly crying as "Softly and Tenderly" is played at the funeral?
a. Lettie Mae.
b. Arlene.
c. Terry.
d. Mike.

23. Who, besides Sookie, stands up to speak at the funeral?
a. Arlene.
b. Lettie Mae.
c. Tara.
d. Terry.

24. Who invited Uncle Bartlett?
a. Sam.

b. Tara.

c. Bill.

d. Jason.

25. Which of the following is not among the traits Sookie lists when describing Adele's hospitality?

a. A warm heart.

b. A hot meal.

c. A shoulder to cry on.

d. A kind word.

26. Why did Lettie Mae attend the funeral?

a. To see Tara.

b. To make peace.

c. Because Adele was kind to her.

d. To get money.

27. How many times did Adele call Social Services on Lettie Mae?

a. One.

b. Two.

c. Three.

d. Four.

28. What does Lettie Mae believe is the source of her problem?

a. Alcohol.

b. Society.

c. Satan.

d. A demon.

29. Who encourages Lettie Mae to attend DGD meetings?

a. Arlene.

b. Tara.

c. Maxine.

d. Everlee.

30. Which of the following is not listed on Bill Compton's gravestone?

a. Husband.

b. Son.

c. Father.
d. Soldier.

31. How does Jason lose the V after the funeral?
a. He drops it.
b. He throws it out the window.
c. It falls behind the seat.
d. It falls out of his pocket.

32. Who returns to the cemetery to walk Sookie home?
a. Tara.
b. Jason.
c. Sam.
d. Arlene.

33. What song is playing as Sookie eats Gran's pie?
a. "Lullaby."
b. "Half of You."
c. "Take Me Home."
d. "We'll Meet Along the Way.

34. Name Tara's neighbor?
a. Roger.
b. John.
c. Travis.
d. Charlie.

35. Tara leaves Lafayette's because he has a webcam in:
a. The bathroom.
b. His bedroom.
c. Her bedroom.
d. Every room.

36. The only thing Tara has to offer Sam is warm:
a. Abita.
b. Dixie.
c. Rolling Rock.
d. Heineken.

37. Sam tells Tara he just wants something _____ in his life.

a. Lasting.

b. Real.

c. True.

d. Special.

38. What is the first thing Sookie does after finishing Gran's pie?

a. Shower.

b. Brush her teeth.

c. Put on nightgown.

d. Read.

39. Where do Sookie and Bill make love for the first time?

a. On the floor.

b. In Bill's bed.

c. In the graveyard.

d. On the sofa.

40. What song plays as Bill and Sookie make love for the first time?

a. "Lullaby."

b. "Half of You."

c. "Take Me Home."

d. "We'll Meet Along the Way."

1.6 Answers

1. A. 2. B. 3. A. 4. B. 5. C. 6. A. 7. B. 8. A. 9. A. 10. C. 11. C. 12. A. 13. D. 14. B. 15. A. 16. B. 17. B. 18. A. 19. D. 20. A. 21. A. 22. C. 23. B. 24. D. 25. A. 26. D. 27. B. 28. D. 29. C. 30. B. 31. B. 32. C. 33. C. 34. A. 35. A. 36. C. 37. B. 38. C. 39. A. 40. B.

1.07 BURNING HOUSE OF LOVE
Written by: Chris Offutt
Directed by: Marcos Siega

1. Which of the following is not a myth Bill debunks while in the bath with Sookie:
a. No reflection.
b. Holy water.
c. Crucifixes.
d. Silver.

2. To balance the effects of their lovemaking, Bill recommends Sookie start taking:
a. Vitamin K.
b. Vitamin B12.
c. Vitamin E.
d. Iron.

3. In a flashback, Uncle Bartlett uses what excuse to get Sookie to sit on his lap?
a. Reading to her.
b. Brushing her hair.
c. Helping with her homework.
d. Tying her shoe.

4. Back in the present, Jason walks in on Lafayette flashing his _____ thong to the webcam.
a. Pink.

b. Red.

c. Gold.

d. Purple.

5. How much does Lettie Mae's exorcism cost?

a. $495.

b. $432.

c. $445.

d. $456.

6. Bill's resting place is concealed under:

a. A rug.

b. A desk.

c. A dresser.

d. A bookshelf.

7. Which of the following does Lettie Mae refuse to attend, because she's not a group person?

a. AA.

b. DGA.

c. Church.

d. Rehab.

8. Tara tells Lettie Mae her demon should:

a. Pick on someone its own size.

b. Find a hobby.

c. Get a job.

d. Stop drinking.

9. Lettie Mae describes her demon as:

a. Vengeful.

b. Angry.

c. Spiteful.

d. Jealous.

10. Adele's candlesticks were a gift from her mother on what occasion?

a. Her 18th birthday.

b. Her 21st birthday.

c. Her wedding.

d. Her high school graduation.

11. Where does Sam live?

a. Kingfisher Apartments.

b. In Merlotte's.

c. Behind Merlotte's.

d. Bon Temps Motel.

12. Who claims to be unboyfriendable?

a. Arlene.

b. Sookie.

c. Tara.

d. Lafayette.

13. Sam injures his hand attempting to repair what?

a. A table.

b. The sink.

c. A counter.

d. A door.

14. What type of screwdriver does Sam need to complete the above repairs?

a. Flathead.

b. Phillips.

c. Robertson.

d. Torx.

15. To prove he is not a bigot, the banker tells Lettie Mae they recently extended a loan to a/an:

a. African American.

b. Vampire American.

c. Jewish American.

d. Homo American.

16. Once they return from the bank, Tara encourages Lettie Mae to:

a. Drink water.

b. Lie down.

c. Throw up.

d. Eat something.

17. Where does Tara hide her money?
a. A Tide box.
b. A Kleenix box.
c. A Brillo Box.
d. A Cheez-It box.

18. To whom does Lafayette refer as pornalicious?
a. Arlene.
b. Tara.
c. Sookie.
d. Jason.

19. How does Lafayette punish Royce?
a. Salting his pie.
b. Peppering his burger.
c. Heating his spoon.
d. Putting Visine in his water.

20. Who rips Sookie's scarf from her neck?
a. Sam.
b. Arlene.
c. Jason.
d. Tara.

21. Which Fangtasia employee asks Jason if he is related to Sookie?
a. Eric.
b. Pam.
c. Ginger.
d. Long Shadow.

22. Bill finds Uncle Bartlett in the act of:
a. Taking out the trash.
b. Bringing in groceries.
c. Watching television.
d. Putting away a hammer.

23. Miss Jeanette compares exorcism to:
a. Graduation.
b. Baptism.

c. Childbirth.

d. Reincarnation.

24. Miss Jeanette's parents were paid in tobacco and _____.

a. Rice.

b. Fish.

c. Beans.

d. Livestock.

25. According to Lettie Mae, in addition to demons, _____ also runs in the family.

a. Alcoholism.

b. Rage.

c. Sexual deviance.

d. Small mindedness.

26. What smartphone does Eric use?

a. iPhone.

b. Blackberry.

c. Sidekick.

d. Droid.

27. To whom does Sookie refer as "dead trash?"

a. Eric.

b. Long Shadow.

c. Diane.

d. Malcolm.

28. Where does Bill leave Uncle Bartlett's body?

a. A river.

b. A field.

c. A car trunk.

d. Under his porch.

29. What does Sam use to defend Sookie from the Monroe vampires?

a. A chain.

b. A beer tap.

c. A wooden handle.

d. A pool cue.

30. Who else comes to Sookie's defense?

a. Jason.

b. Terry.

c. Hoyt.

d. Lafayette.

31. What is Amy's last name?

a. Burns.

b. Burnett.

c. Burley.

d. Burke.

32. Where is she from?

a. New York.

b. Connecticut.

c. New Hampshire.

d. Vermont.

33. Jason tells Amy he is a _____ doctor.

a. Leg.

b. Boob.

c. Butt.

d. Chick.

34. What is the place of origin of Miss Jeanette's crone stone?

a. Jamaica.

b. Haiti.

c. Africa.

d. New Orleans.

35. How many children are there in Miss Jeanette's generation?

a. 12.

b. 15.

c. 18.

d. 23.

36. The demon allegedly travels from Lettie Mae to a/an:

a. Raccoon.

b. Opossum.

c. Rat.

d. Armadillo.

37. How far is the closest vampire nest to town?

a. One mile.

b. Two miles.

c. Three miles.

d. Four miles.

38. Where did Amy attend college?

a. Smith.

b. Vassar.

c. Wellesley.

d. William and Mary.

39. What did Jason study at the Vo Tech?

a. Auto body repair.

b. Landscape technology.

c. Motorcycle maintenance.

d. Construction management.

40. Andy's ringtone is the theme song of what television show?

a. *Baretta.*

b. *Magnum PI.*

c. *Dragnet.*

d. *Hawaii* 5-0.

1.7 Answers

1. D. 2. B. 3. C. 4. C. 5. C. 6. A. 7. A. 8. C. 9. D. 10. C. 11. C. 12. C. 13. C. 14. C. 15. B. 16. A. 17. C. 18. C. 19. C. 20. A. 21. B. 22. A. 23. C. 24. D. 25. C. 26. C. 27. D. 28. A. 29. D. 30. B. 31. C. 32. B. 33. A. 34. C. 35. A. 36. B. 37. D. 38. C. 39. B. 40. D.

1.08 THE FOURTH MAN IN THE FIRE
Written by: Alexander Woo
Directed by: Michael Lehmann

1. How many sets of vampire remains are there in the fire?
a. Two.
b. Three.
c. Four.
d. Five.

2. Tara is awoken just before _____ to the sound of Lettie Mae throwing out bottles.
a. 6:00am.
b. 7:00am.
c. 8:00am.
d. 9:00am.

3. For breakfast, Lettie Mae makes bacon and:
a. Hoe cakes.
b. Eggs.
c. Biscuits.
d. Grits.

4. What does Sookie do upon returning home after Bill's "death"?
a. Clean.
b. Bathe.
c. Sleep.
d. Scream.

5. What type of pizza does Jason eat for breakfast?
a. Pepperoni blast.
b. Pepperoni and sausage.
c. Meat lovers.
d. Mushroom and olive.

6. How did Jason's parents die?
a. Tornado.
b. Hurricane.
c. Flash flood.
d. Fire.

7. How old was Jason when his parents died?
a. Almost ten.
b. Almost eleven.
c. Almost twelve.
d. Almost thirteen.

8. Around his neck, Terry wears the penis of what creature?
a. Raccoon.
b. Opossum.
c. Rat.
d. Armadillo.

9. Amy compares Merlotte's to what type of museum?
a. Natural history.
b. Louisiana history.
c. Modern art.
d. Children's.

10. Sookie tells Arlene that she loves her, even if she is a/an:
a. Space cadet.
b. Jesus freak.
c. Bigot.
d. Airhead.

11. How are the tables in Merlotte's numbered:
a. Left to right.
b. Right to left.

c. Clockwise.

d. Counterclockwise.

12. Who walks Lettie Mae home from church?

a. Maxine.

b. Everlee.

c. Rosie.

d. Mabel.

13. How long has it been since Lettie Mae's last church visit?

a. A year.

b. Two years.

c. Three years.

d. Four years.

14. Terry offers to babysit for Arlene, telling her that he loves kids and

_____.

a. Pizza.

b. Cookies.

c. Hot dogs.

d. Donuts.

15. To earn extra money, Amy makes:

a. Dresses.

b. Cakes.

c. Jewelry.

d. Dolls.

16. The tattoo on Terry's left bicep reads:

a. USMC.

b. Death Before Dishonor.

c. Semper Fi.

d. Never Forget.

17. Sookie babysits Arlene's children so that she can attend the concert of a/an _____ tribute band.

a. Statler Brothers.

b. Oak Ridge Boys.

c. Alabama.

d. Gatlin Brothers.

18. At what time does Arlene drop the children at Sookie's?

a. 6:00pm.

b. 7:00pm.

c. 8:00pm.

d. 9:00pm.

19. Bill tells Sookie the beauty and the tragedy is that she doesn't know how
_____ she is.

a. Unique.

b. Special.

c. Different.

d. Extraordinary.

20. How many voicemails did Bill receive from Sookie the night of the fire?

a. One.

b. Two.

c. Three.

d. Four.

21. What excuse does Sookie give for being late to answer the door when
Arlene arrives?

a. The cat got out.

b. She was in the bathroom.

c. The T.V. was too loud.

d. She was on the phone.

22. What do Bill and Sookie feed the kids?

a. Grilled cheese.

b. Hot dogs.

c. Hamburgers.

d. Pizza.

23. When pressed to give a flaw, Sam tells Tara that she _____ in her sleep.

a. Talks.

b. Grunts.

c. Groans.

d. Mumbles.

24. Bill tells the children he doesn't eat the pizza because he is:

a. Still full from dinner.

b. Lactose intolerant.

c. Diabetic.

d. Allergic to garlic.

25. Lisa tells Bill he should give Sookie:

a. Flowers.

b. Chocolate.

c. Jewelry.

d. A valentine.

26. Where does Rene hide Arlene's engagement ring?

a. Her coin purse.

b. His lunch box.

c. A flashlight.

d. A coffee mug.

27. How many times has Arlene been married?

a. One.

b. Two.

c. Three.

d. Four.

28. Who is revealed to be the fourth set of remains in the fire?

a. JB.

b. Neil.

c. Royce.

d. Mike.

29. How old was Bud when he worked at a slaughterhouse?

a. 14.

b. 15.

c. 16.

d. 17.

30. Sam tells Andy his parents were naturists outside:
a. Beaumont.
b. Port Arthur.
c. Jasper.
d. Deweyville.

31. The naturist facility in question has records that date back to:
a. 1948.
b. 1958.
c. 1968.
d. 1978.

32. Lafayette tells Tara that the cost of the exorcism is a bargain compared to a life on:
a. Prozac.
b. Ativan.
c. Zoloft.
d. Xanax.

33. Upon returning home, Bill finds Eric waiting in his:
a. Kitchen.
b. Living room.
c. Dining room.
d. Bathroom.

34. On what evening do Eddie and Lafayette meet weekly?
a. Monday.
b. Tuesday.
c. Wednesday.
d. Thursday.

35. Eric is the sheriff of Area:
a. Three.
b. Four.
c. Five.
d. Six.

36. Sookie dreams of sharing what daylight activity with Bill?
a. Tanning.

b. Swinging on the porch.

c. Playing with children.

d. Eating breakfast.

37. How much money is missing from Fangtasia's books?

a. $300,000.

b. $400,000.

c. $500,000.

d. $600,000.

38. What is the first name of Fangtasia's accountant?

a. Bradley.

b. Bruce.

c. Brian.

d. Bobby.

39. What does Lafayette drive?

a. Lexus.

b. Mercedes.

c. Audi.

d. BMW.

40. When Amy and Jason come to Eddie's door, he is watching:

a. *Phang Tales.*

b. *Phang Fans.*

c. *Fang Philes.*

d. *Phangs.*

1.8 Answers

1. B. 2. C. 3. A. 4. A. 5. B. 6. C. 7. B. 8. B. 9. A. 10. C. 11. C. 12. D. 13. B. 14. D. 15. C. 16. A. 17. B. 18. C. 19. C. 20. C. 21. A. 22. D. 23. B. 24. B. 25. A. 26. C. 27. D. 28. B. 29. B. 30. A. 31. B. 32. C. 33. D. 34. A. 35. C. 36. D. 37. D. 38. B. 39. B. 40. C.

1.09 PLAISIR D'AMOUR
Written by: Brian Buckner
Directed by: Anthony M. Hemingway

1. With what does Bill stake Long Shadow?
a. A beer tap.
b. A pool cue.
c. A chair leg.
d. A cabinet handle.

2. According to Eric, Tru:Blood's slogan should be that it keeps you alive:
a. But it tastes like death.
b. But you will wish you weren't.
c. If you can stand to drink it.
d. But it will bore you to death.

3. Jason states that he should've know there was something wrong based upon the size of Amy's:
a. Jewelry.
b. Shoes.
c. Bag.
d. Eyes.

4. Where do Jason and Amy imprison Eddie?
a. A shed.
b. An abandoned house.
c. A basement.
d. An empty office.

5. To restrain Eddie, they tie him to:
a. A table.
b. A chair.
c. A shelf.
d. A cabinet.

6. Why does Amy cut V with aspirin?
a. To minimize head rush.
b. To ease its entry into the system.
c. To lower blood pressure.
d. To prevent clotting.

7. Miss Jeanette tells Tara her _____ is sick.
a. Head.
b. Heart.
c. Psyche.
d. Soul.

8. What is the cost of Tara's exorcism?
a. $699.95.
b. $799.95.
c. $899.95.
d. $999.95.

9. From whom does Tara get the money for her exorcism?
a. Lettie Mae.
b. Sookie.
c. Sam.
d. Lafayette.

10. Which vampire is said to treat every day like it is Halloween?
a. Bill.
b. Eric.
c. Pam.
d. Eddie.

11. Where does Sookie find her dead cat?
a. Her bed.
b. The ceiling fan.

c. The refrigerator.
d. On the stove.

12. Amy finds _____ that Jason bought after 9/11.
a. Gas masks.
b. Bottled water.
c. A bullet proof vest.
d. MRE rations.

13. In an effort to clean Jason's diet, Amy feeds him:
a. Blueberries.
b. Almonds.
c. Tofu.
d. Sunflower seeds.

14. Who compares feeding a vampire to putting gas in a car?
a. Royce.
b. JB.
c. Rene.
d. Jason.

15. Why does Lettie Mae assume Tara is sleeping with Sam?
a. He calls her constantly.
b. She put on makeup.
c. He brought her flowers.
d. She hasn't been home all week.

16. Which of the following does Sam not agree to cover for Arlene's engagement party?
a. Band.
b. Alcohol.
c. Catering.
d. Decorations.

17. Lafayette is disgusted by the mayonnaise on his burger from:
a. Yippo's.
b. Yano's.
c. Yako's.
d. Yukko's.

18. Who does Jason attack to save a tree?
a. Hoyt.
b. Lafayette.
c. Rene.
d. JB.

19. What is Andy's standard order at Merlotte's?
a. Burger and fries.
b. Catfish nuggets.
c. Oyster po' boy.
d. Chicken strips and onion rings.

20. Jason takes great offense when who calls him "J?"
a. Hoyt.
b. Lafayette.
c. Rene.
d. JB.

21. They are not allowed to call him that because they are not what?
a. His mama.
b. His gran.
c. His sister.
d. His teammate.

22. What souvenir did Tina's killer choose to keep?
a. Tail.
b. Head.
c. Heart.
d. Paw.

23. What gaming system does Bill own?
a. Playstation.
b. X Box.
c. Wii.
d. Nintendo DS.

24. Bill and Chow compare scores on what course?
a. Gleneagle.
b. St. Andrews.

c. Pine Valley.

d. Pebble Beach.

25. What is Bill's best score?

a. Five under.

b. Seven under.

c. Nine under.

d. Eleven under.

26. What is Chow's best score?

a. Five under.

b. Seven under.

c. Nine under.

d. Eleven under.

27. What is Chow's position at Fangtasia?

a. Bodyguard.

b. Bartender.

c. Doorman.

d. Cook.

28. Before leaving for the tribunal, Bill asks to stop at:

a. His house.

b. Sookie's house.

c. Merlotte's.

d. Fangtasia.

29. What was Eddie's occupation before he became a vampire?

a. Lawyer.

b. Telemarketer.

c. Accountant.

d. Office manager.

30. Why did Eddie become a vampire?

a. To attract men.

b. To live forever.

c. To escape his boredom.

d. Because he couldn't think of a reason not to.

31. Who does Bill ask to look after Sookie in his absence?
a. Jason.
b. Eric.
c. Lafayette.
d. Sam.

32. What night is Ladies' Night at Fangtasia?
a. Monday.
b. Tuesday.
c. Wednesday.
d. Thursday.

33. Eric allows Bill _____ minutes to speak to Sookie before leaving.
a. Two.
b. Three.
c. Four.
d. Five.

34. Witnessing Bill and Sookie, Pam says that if she had any feelings, she would:
a. Have the chills.
b. Cry blood tears.
c. Give a damn.
d. Be touched.

35. Eddie tells Jason he has not yet learned to:
a. Glamour.
b. Levitate.
c. Change form.
d. Turn another vampire.

36. Who first identified Eddie as gay?
a. A coworker.
b. His wife.
c. His wife's friend.
d. His child(ren)'s friend.

37. How many children did Eddie have?
a. None.

b. One.

c. Two.

d. Three.

38. Who does Sookie tell she will be spending the night at Bill's?

a. Tara.

b. Arlene.

c. Sam.

d. Amy.

39. While attempting to follow Sookie, Sam is briefly detained by whom?

a. Terry.

b. Arlene.

c. Tara.

d. Andy.

40. What does Sookie name Sam in dog form?

a. Dirk.

b. Dino.

c. Dean.

d. Doug.

1.9 Answers

1. A. 2. D. 3. C. 4. C. 5. B. 6. D. 7. D. 8. B. 9. C. 10. C. 11. B. 12. A. 13. B. 14. D. 15. C. 16. D. 17. B. 18. C. 19. A. 20. A. 21. D. 22. B. 23. C. 24. D. 25. B. 26. D. 27. B. 28. C. 29. C. 30. A. 31. D. 32. D. 33. B. 34. A. 35. A. 36. D. 37. B. 38. D. 39. D. 40. C.

1.10 I DON'T WANNA KNOW
Written by: Chris Offutt
Directed by: Scott Winant

1. Where does Tara's exorcism occur?
a. Miss Jeanette's trailor.
b. In the woods.
c. In a parking lot.
d. In a field.

2. Miss Jeanette tells Tara that _____ root and spit are stronger than holy water.
a. Angelica.
b. Unicorn.
c. Gravel.
d. Pleurisy.

3. What does Miss Jeanette tell Tara is/are the demon's doorway?
a. Eyes.
b. Heart.
c. Mouth.
d. Stomach.

4. Amy walked away from an academic scholarship to volunteer where?
a. Columbia.
b. Guatemala.
c. Peru.
d. Ecuador.

5. In what year of college did it occur?

a. Freshman.

b. Sophomore.

c. Junior.

d. Senior.

6. Who tells Amy that Jason isn't as evolved as she is?

a. Sookie.

b. Arlene.

c. Andy.

d. Eddie.

7. Why are dogs the easiest change for Sam?

a. People like dogs.

b. Dogs are emotional.

c. Dogs are loyal.

d. Dogs' anatomies are similar.

8. What animal does Sam say is too complex?

a. Fish.

b. Bird.

c. Wolf.

d. Human.

9. Which supernatural creature is not referenced in this episode?

a. Vampire.

b. Werewolf.

c. Witch.

d. Shifter.

10. Miss Jeanette tells Tara she is drinking _____ juice.

a. Bat.

b. Scorpion.

c. Snake.

d. Tarantula.

11. What form does the demon take?

a. Opossum.

b. Eagle.

c. Child.

d. Cat.

12. With what disease/disorder does Amy hope to inflict Eddie?

a. Stockholm Syndrome.

b. Paranoia.

c. Schizophrenia.

d. Chemical dependency.

13. Why is Jason intrigued by Amy's travel plans?

a. He's never left Louisiana.

b. He's never seen snow.

c. He's never been to Disney World.

d. He's never taken a road trip.

14. Where do Lettie Mae and Tara go to celebrate her exorcism?

a. MeeMaw's Mudbugs.

b. Mama's Mudbugs.

c. Mammy's Mudbugs.

d. Mamaw's Mudbugs.

15. What does Arlene ask Sam to rearrange at the last minute?

a. The seating.

b. The lanterns.

c. The flowers.

d. The chairs.

16. Name Terry's debutante cousin.

a. Jessica.

b. Amelia.

c. Portia.

d. Anabelle.

17. Every female Bellefleur has been a debutante since before the:

a. Revolutionary War.

b. Civil War.

c. First World War.

d. War of 1812.

18. On what dog did Sam first imprint?

a. Collie.

b. Beagle.

c. Cocker spaniel.

d. Lab.

19. Senator Finch's visit interrupts Lafayette in the process of what?

a. Painting his toenails.

b. Shaving his legs.

c. Waxing his chest.

d. Bleaching his lip.

20. Where does Miss Jeanette work?

a. Stina's.

b. Wall Drug.

c. De Soto Pharmacy.

d. Super Sav-A-Bunch.

21. What is Miss Jeanette's first name?

a. Nancy.

b. Mary.

c. Cass.

d. Shannon.

22. Miss Jeanette has a daughter with what disease?

a. IBS.

b. Autism.

c. Epilepsy.

d. Diabetes.

23. Miss Jeanette reveals that the concoction she gave Tara was actually _____ and peyote.

a. Midazolam syrup.

b. Ipecac syrup.

c. Albuterol syrup.

d. Hycodan syrup.

24. The band at Arlene's party is lead by whom?

a. Jace Everett.

b. Nathan Barr.

c. CC Adcock.

d. Paul Cebar.

25. What does Terry tell Sookie is a useless emotion?

a. Jealousy.

b. Anger.

c. Depression.

d. Guilt.

26. How long does it take fangs to grow back?

a. Six months.

b. Five months.

c. Four months.

d. Three months.

27. Removal of fangs is the punishment for what offense?

a. Killing a vampire.

b. Feeding on another's human.

c. Killing another's human.

d. Siding with a human over a vampire.

28. Maxine reprimands Hoyt for consuming how many beers?

a. Two.

b. Three.

c. Four.

d. Five.

29. The Magister was trained during:

a. The Holocaust.

b. The Crusades.

c. The Inquisition.

d. The Nika Riots.

30. The Magister's territory covers what geographic region?

a. All of Area 5.

b. All of Louisiana.

c. All of North America.

d. All of the Western Hemisphere.

31. The usual punishment for staking a vampire is to be chained in a coffin for how long?
a. Five years.
b. Ten years.
c. Fifteen years.
d. Twenty years.

32. Who describes Arlene's dating history as a series of "fixer uppers?"
a. Sookie.
b. Sam.
c. Lafayette.
d. Arlene.

33. What year was Tara's prom?
a. 2000.
b. 2001.
c. 2002.
d. 2003.

34. Sam has been on his own since he was:
a. 14.
b. 15.
c. 16.
d. 17.

35. Who confronts Jason at Arlene's party?
a. Sookie.
b. Tara.
c. Andy.
d. Lafayette.

36. Jessica was kidnapped on her way to whose party?
a. Ashley's.
b. Brittney's.
c. Chloe's.
d. Missy's.

37. Sookie is attacked by the killer when she goes into Merlotte's for what?
a. Beer.

b. Snacks.

c. Ice.

d. Cups.

38. Tara crashes her car after seeing a naked lady with what animal?

a. Dog.

b. Pig.

c. Horse.

d. Bull.

39. According to the Magister, humans are incapable of feeling:

a. Guilt.

b. Emotion.

c. Pain.

d. Enlightened.

40. Jessica asks Bill if he is:

a. A monster.

b. A vampire.

c. A dream.

d. A Christian.

1.10 Answers

1. B. 2. A. 3. A. 4. B. 5. B. 6. D. 7. A. 8. D. 9. C. 10. C. 11. C 12. A. 13. B. 14. D. 15. B. 16. C. 17. A. 18. B. 19. C. 20. C. 21. A. 22. D. 23. B. 24. C. 25. D. 26. D. 27. B. 28. B. 29. C. 30. C. 31. A. 32. D. 33. A. 34. B. 35. D. 36. A. 37. C. 38. B. 39. C. 40. D.

1.11 TO LOVE IS TO BURY
Written and Directed by: Nancy Oliver

1. Who accompanies Bill to make sure doesn't stake Jessica before she goes to ground?
a. Eric.
b. Pam.
c. The Magister.
d. Stan.

2. The above vampire refers to humans as pathetic lumps of _____ flesh.
a. Fleeting.
b. Transitory.
c. Transient.
d. Temporary.

3. How does Sookie describe the killer's thoughts?
a. Red and black.
b. Black and fuzzy.
c. Gray and fuzzy.
d. Red and emotional.

4. From the mind of the killer, Sookie remembers that the victim was wearing _____ and a name tag.
a. Tennis shoes.
b. A wedding ring.
c. An apron.
d. Red nail polish.

5. What was the victim's name?
a. Cindy.
b. Carrie.
c. Candy.
d. Corie.

6. Who interrogates Tara after the accident?
a. Andy.
b. Kenya.
c. Kevin.
d. Bud.

7. What is the title of the officer listed above?
a. Sheriff.
b. Sheriff's Deputy.
c. Detective.
d. Sargeant.

8. Amy tries to justify her actions by saying that Eddie was not a man, he was a:
a. Monster.
b. Cannibal.
c. Predator.
d. Parasite.

9. What is Sookie reading when Sam comes to breakfast?
a. Phone book.
b. Newspaper.
c. Scrapbook.
d. A box of letters.

10. Pam likens being a maker to being what?
a. A god.
b. A hero.
c. Royalty.
d. A parent.

11. Big Patty's Pie Shop is near what neighboring city?
a. Shreveport.

b. Monroe.

c. Marthaville.

d. Bunkie.

12. Where does Amy dispose of Eddie?

a. The garbage disposal.

b. The flower bed.

c. The trash can.

d. The freezer.

13. What is Lafayette in the process of doing when he sees Finch on television?

a. Painting his toenails.

b. Shaving his legs.

c. Waxing his chest.

d. Bleaching his lip.

14. Finch's anti-vampire platform alleges that V will turn children into all of the following, except which?

a. Addicts.

b. Drug dealers.

c. Sex fiends.

d. Homosexuals.

15. What channel is Lafayette watching at the time?

a. WWJC.

b. KKJH.

c. WDAC.

d. KFBG.

16. Who claims an inability to watch politicians because they get seizures?

a. Terry.

b. Bud.

c. Andy.

d. Kevin.

17. Which of the following was included in the pies ordered for Sam and Sookie at Big Patty's?

a. Snickers.

b. Chocolate pecan.

c. Peanut butter.

d. Lemon Meringue.

18. Name the patron that orders for Sam and Sookie.

a. Buster.

b. Buddy.

c. Bucky.

d. Barkley.

19. The deceased Big Patty's waitress had moved into town just over:

a. One year ago.

b. Two years ago.

c. Three years ago.

d. Four years ago.

20. What was her brother's name?

a. Dave Marshall.

b. Doug Marshall.

c. Dean Marshall.

d. Drew Marshall.

21. To whom does Tara make her jail phone call?

a. Lettie Mae.

b. Sam.

c. Lafayette.

d. Jason.

22. Sookie overhears the police officer thinking about an affair with whom

a. Denise.

b. Debbie.

c. Dottie.

d. Dana.

23. Where does Lafayette go to confront Finch?

a. Hotel Orleans.

b. St. Charles Hotel.

c. Remington Hotel.

d. Delacroix Hotel.

24. When it is all over, Sookie says, she wants to:
a. Dance in the street.
b. Rent a convertible.
c. Go to Florida.
d. Eat for a week.

25. When Sookie jokes about Sam sticking his head out the window, he replies that it is:
a. A private pleasure.
b. Not as much fun as it looks.
c. Overrated.
d. A myth.

26. How much V do Jason and Amy split on their last night together?
a. One vial.
b. One vial each.
c. One drop each.
d. One drop total.

27. Which of the following is not a reason Bill gives Jessica for her being made vampire?
a. She was unlucky.
b. Life is unfair.
c. Fate is fickle.
d. Because of Bill.

28. What instrument does Jessica play?
a. Clarinet.
b. Cello.
c. Piano.
d. Flute.

29. Which of the following is not included in Jessica's list of the pros of being a vampire?
a. No more belts.
b. No more schools.
c. No more rules.
d. She can curse.

30. Lettie Mae took her time visiting Tara in jail because she was praying with whom?
a. Maxine.
b. Everlee.
c. Rosie.
d. Mabel.

31. Who pays Tara's bail?
a. Maryann.
b. Lettie Mae.
c. Sam.
d. Lafayette.

32. With what was Amy strangled?
a. A scarf.
b. A belt.
c. A phone cord.
d. A shirt.

33. Who answers the phone at the police department when Eric calls to turn himself in?
a. Bud.
b. Andy.
c. Kenya.
d. Rosie.

34. Maryann is well known by which employee of the Bon Temps Police Department?
a. Bud.
b. Andy.
c. Kenya.
d. Rosie.

35. Tara mistakes Maryann for what?
a. A social worker.
b. A drug counselor.
c. A lawyer.
d. A preacher.

36. With what does Sookie hit Bill, to get him off Sam?

a. Bottle.

b. Vase.

c. Chair.

d. Book.

37. How much time does Andy claim he needs alone with Jason in order to obtain a confession?

a. Two minutes.

b. Five minutes.

c. Ten minutes.

d. Fifteen minutes.

38. Andy threatens to use what interrogation technique(s)?

a. Chinese water torture.

b. The rack.

c. Waterboarding.

d. All of the above.

39. Who claims to not be a "Jesus" person?

a. Jason.

b. Tara.

c. Maryann.

d. Lafayette.

40. The fax containing the killer's face is not seen, because it is covered with files. By whom?

a. Andy.

b. Bud.

c. Kenya.

d. Rosie.

1.11 Answers

1. B. 2. D. 3. A. 4. C. 5. A. 6. B. 7. B. 8. C. 9. A. 10. B. 11. D. 12. A. 13. A. 14. C. 15. B. 16. A. 17. C. 18. A. 19. B. 20. D. 21. A. 22. B. 23. C. 24. B. 25. A. 26. D. 27. C. 28. A. 29. B. 30. D. 31. A. 32. B. 33. D. 34. C. 35. A. 36. B. 37. B. 38. C. 39. C. 40. D.

1.12 YOU'LL BE THE DEATH OF ME
Written by: Raelle Tucker
Directed by: Alan Ball

1. When it appears he is going to be sentenced, Jason gives away his most prized possessions. What does he give Hoyt?
a. His jacket.
b. His tools.
c. His shotgun.
d. His Playboy collection.

2. What does he leave Sookie?
a. His house.
b. His bank account.
c. His house and bank account.
d. None of the above.

3. To whom does he give his truck?
a. Rene.
b. Lafayette.
c. Hoyt.
d. Amy's parents.

4. Who tries to keep Sookie from visiting Jason in jail?
a. Andy.
b. Bud.
c. Kevin.
d. Kenya.

5. What type of artwork can be found on Tara's bedroom walls at Maryann's?
a. Landscapes.
b. Still lifes.
c. Nudes.
d. Graffiti.

6. Tara claims her breakfast isn't food, it's:
a. Magic.
b. Heaven.
c. Art.
d. Sculpture.

7. Maryann tells Tara her situation is an opportunity to do what?
a. Rebuild.
b. Regroup.
c. Reevaluate.
d. Recharge.

8. Carl turns off Tara's phone when she receives an incoming call from whom?
a. Sookie.
b. Lettie Mae.
c. Sam.
d. Lafayette.

9. Jason is informed the Fellowship of the Sun has developed a fund for:
a. A scholarship in his name.
b. Support of his loved ones, should he not get out.
c. Him to join the Fellowship.
d. His defense.

10. In what activity is Eggs engaged when he and Tara meet for the first time?
a. Smoking.
b. Eating.
c. Playing guitar.
d. Swimming.

11. What was Tara drinking when she crashed?
a. Bourbon.

b. Scotch.

c. Rum.

d. Vodka.

12. Lafayette refers to something that is too good to be true as what?

a. Satan in a Sunday hat.

b. A werewolf in sheep's clothing.

c. A gift horse with a big mouth.

d. Counting your chickens before their fried.

13. Rene sings along to what song while driving the truck to Merlotte's?

a. "Paint it Black."

b. "Don't Fear the Reaper."

c. "Devil in Disguise."

d. "Thriller."

14. Rene tells Sookie he'll have a friend from Auto _____ look at her car.

a. Mall.

b. Barn.

c. Alley.

d. Haven.

15. Arlene walks in on Cody and Lisa watching a sex tape of a vampire and whom?

a. Maudette.

b. Dawn.

c. Sookie.

d. Rene's sister.

16. Rene tells Sookie her house is hotter than what?

a. A firecracker's ass.

b. Hell on a Sunday.

c. A whorehouse in July.

d. A horseradish.

17. Sam realizes Rene is the killer when he smell's Rene's:

a. Vest.

b. Hat.

c. Glove.

d. Belt.

18. How much of a lead do Rene and Sookie have on Sam according to Terry?

a. 5-8 minutes.

b. 10-13 minutes.

c. 15-18 minutes.

d. 20-23 minutes.

19. What does Sookie drop when she realizes Rene is the killer?

a. A vase.

b. A pitcher.

c. A glass.

d. A carton of milk.

20. Sookie escapes the house by hitting Rene with what?

a. A gun.

b. A vase.

c. A mirror.

d. A shovel.

21. Where is Sookie hiding when Rene finds her?

a. Behind a tree.

b. Under the truck.

c. Behind a tombstone.

d. In a grave.

22. To protect him from the sunlight, Bill is buried in the open grave of whom?

a. Sylvia Bellefleur.

b. Sadie Bellefleur.

c. Sophia Bellefleur.

d. Suzette Bellefleur.

23. Sookie is able to briefly turn the tables on Rene. Why?

a. His is distracted by Sam.

b. He is distracted by Bill.

c. He thinks she is dead.

d. He has a flashback to his sister.

24. How many women had Drew Marshall killed by the end of his reign?

a. Three.

b. Four.

c. Five.

d. Six.

25. What are the only words Bill is able to speak before losing consciousness?

a. I love you.

b. I am sorry.

c. I failed you.

d. You are safe.

26. Who among the following is not present when Sookie wakes?

a. Sam.

b. Tara.

c. Lafayette.

d. Arlene.

27. When Jason asks Andy if his release is a trick, Andy responds that it is what?

a. A travesty.

b. An injustice.

c. A joke.

d. A miracle.

28. When she sees Sam, Maryann refers to him as a _____ dog.

a. Mangy.

b. Dirty.

c. Silly.

d. Crazy.

29. Which of the following is not on the list of things Jason thought he was good at prior to going to jail?

a. Football.

b. Drinking.

c. Chasing women.

d. Thinking about himself.

30. On the way out of the house, Jason trips over what?

a. Chair.

b. Footstool.

c. Coffee table.

d. Coat rack.

31. Who is Sookie watching on television when Bill returns?

a. Judy Garland.

b. Shirley Temple.

c. Laurel and Hardy.

d. Abbot and Costello.

32. Why does Sookie refuse Bill's blood?

a. There will be time for that later.

b. She just wants to be held.

c. She wants to feel human.

d. She owes him enough already.

33. How long will it take Sookie to heal without Bill's blood?

a. Days.

b. Weeks.

c. Months.

d. Years.

34. Why does Sookie cut short Bill's apology?

a. Her life is too short.

b. He doesn't owe her any apology.

c. She should be apologizing to him.

d. She just needs silence.

35. What state is the first to legalize human/vampire marriage?

a. California.

b. Vermont.

c. Massachusetts.

d. New York.

36. How much time passes between Bill's return and the first state legalizing human/vampire marriage?
a. A week.
b. Two weeks.
c. Three weeks.
d. A month.

37. Tara tells Sam he is a subtle as what?
a. A flying brick.
b. A box of hammers.
c. A bull in a china shop.
d. A Jew at an Al Qaida rally.

38. What family previously owned the land on which Merlotte's now stands?
a. Stackhouse.
b. Compton.
c. Bellefleur.
d. Thornton.

39. What is Bill doing when Eric and Pam return Jessica?
a. Playing Wii.
b. Reading.
c. Playing the piano.
d. Watching tv.

40. Who does Sookie call to pick up Andy?
a. Portia.
b. Terry.
c. Caroline.
d. Bud.

1.12 Answers

1. A. 2. C. 3. A. 4. C. 5. C. 6. D. 7. A. 8. C. 9. D. 10. C. 11. D. 12. A. 13. C. 14. D. 15. A. 16. B. 17. A. 18. D. 19. B. 20. A. 21. D. 22. C. 23. A. 24. C. 25. B. 26. D. 27. D. 28. C. 29. A. 30. C. 31. B. 32. C. 33. B. 34. A. 35. B. 36. B. 37. A. 38. C. 39. C. 40. A.

SEASON TWO
2.01 NOTHING BUT THE BLOOD
Written by: Alexander Woo
Directed by: Daniel Minahan

1. Where is Miss Jeanette's body found?
a. The Merlotte's dumpster.
b. The Merlotte's freezer.
c. Andy Bellefleur's car.
d. Arlene Fowler's car.

2. What color were the victim's toenails?
a. Pink.
b. Red.
c. Purple.
d. Green.

3. How did they know instantly that she was dead?
a. She had no pulse.
b. She had a stake through her heart.
c. She had no heart.
d. She had no head.

4. Andy cites full rigor mortis as evidence that the victim:
a. Was killed elsewhere.
b. Was killed violently.
c. Was killed days earlier.
d. All of the above.

5. All of the following were present when the body was found, except whom?
a. Andy.
b. Sookie.
c. Tara.
d. Arlene.

6. At what time had Andy clocked in that morning?
a. 6:00 AM.
b. 7:00 AM.
c. 8:00AM.
d. 9:00AM.

7. What does Bill establish as Jessica Hamby's bedtime?
a. 4:00 AM.
b. 4:30 AM.
c. 5:00 AM.
d. 5:30 AM.

8. Per the Compton recycling policy, Tru:Blood bottles are placed in which bin?
a. Green.
b. White.
c. Blue.
d. Brown.

9. Bill orders Jessica to change, so that she doesn't look like…
a. A prostitute.
b. A slattern.
c. A tart.
d. A whore.

10. While reading a book provided by the Fellowship, Jason quotes which book of the Bible?
a. Job.
b. Acts of the Apostles.
c. Genesis.
d. Revelations.

11. What is Miss Jeanette's real name?

a. Nancy LeGuar.

b. Nancy Lenier.

c. Nancy Devereaux.

d. Nancy LeFevre.

12. Where was Lafayette on the night of Miss Jeanette's murder?

a. Merlotte's.

b. Fangtasia

c. With a client.

d. At home.

13. Lafayette was soon joined by whom?

a. Mike.

b. Royce.

c. JB.

d. Hoyt.

14. Immediately before meeting Sookie, Jessica was engaged in what activity?

a. Feeding.

b. Showering.

c. Sleeping.

d. Hunting.

15. Maryann accuses whom of neglecting Tara?

a. Sookie.

b. Sam.

c. Lafayette.

d. Lettie Mae.

16. What make of car does Maryann drive?

a. BMW.

b. Porsche.

c. Jaguar.

d. Lexus.

17. How old was Jessica at the time of her death?

a. 16.

b. 17.

c. 18.
d. 19.

18. How many weeks passed between the turning of Jessica and its revelation to Sookie?
a. A week.
b. Two weeks.
c. Three weeks.
d. A month.

19. Including Jessica, how many vampires has Bill turned?
a. One.
b. Two.
c. Three.
d. Four.

20. Where is Nan Flanagan during her live interview with Steve Newlin?
a. Beijing.
b. Hong Kong.
c. New Delhi.
d. Tokyo.

21. What was Steve Newlin's father's name?
a. Steven.
b. Theodore.
c. Robert.
d. Jeremiah.

22. On what network did the Newlin/ Flanagan interview air?
a. CNN.
b. BTNN.
c. VNN.
d. TBBN.

23. Sarah Newlin believes her husband has the potential to hold what public office?
a. Mayor of Dallas.
b. Governor of Texas.

c. Senator.

d. President.

24. Who introduces Jason to the Newlins?

a. Sid Matt Lancaster.

b. JB DuRone.

c. Orry Dodson.

d. Luke McDonald.

25. How long was Lafayette in captivity?

a. Four days.

b. One week.

c. Two weeks.

d. One month.

26. The Light of Day Institute, to which Jason is invited, is described as:

a. A leadership conference.

b. A spiritual retreat.

c. A spiritual awakening.

d. Jesus boot camp.

27. What is the fee to attend LODI?

a. $1000.

b. $1100.

c. $1200.

d. $1300.

28. Sam finds a replica of what ancient statue in Maryann's home?

a. Venus of Lespugue.

b. Bird Lady.

c. Statue of an Old Market Woman.

d. Minoan Snake Goddess.

29. The original statue is located in which New York museum?

a. The Brooklyn Museum.

b. The Guggenheim Museum.

c. The Metropolitan Museum of Art.

d. The Whitney Museum.

30. How old was Sam when he met Maryann for the first time?
a. 14.
b. 15.
c. 16.
d. 17.

31. Prior to learning of Uncle Bartlett's fate, Sookie is listening over breakfast?
a. Hello, Darlin.
b. Hello, Walls.
c. Hello, Goodbye.
d. Hello, I Love You.

32. Who delivers the news of Uncle Bartlett's death?
a. Mike Spencer.
b. Reverand White.
c. Andy Bellefleur.
d. Sid Matt Lancaster.

33. Whose likeness is painted by Maryann's pool?
a. Bacchus.
b. Aphrodite.
c. Pan.
d. Daphne.

34. Maryann hits Carl because he brought unnecessary:
a. Fruit.
b. Flowers.
c. Drinks.
d. Towels.

35. Royce states that he has a magnetic:
a. Head.
b. Johnson.
c. Foot.
d. Ass.

36. Prior to coming to Merlotte's, Daphne waited tables at:
a. Cracker Barrel.

b. Waffle House.

c. IHOP.

d. Sizzler.

37. Who claims that Maxine Fortenberry has "more chins than a Chinese phonebook?"

a. Tara.

b. Jane.

c. Maryann.

d. Arlene.

38. What fictional church does Jason give as the sponsor of his retreat?

a. Seagrams Methodist.

b. Marlboro Baptist.

c. Michelob Methodist.

d. Winston Baptist.

39. When not protecting the citizens of Bon Temps, Bud Dearborn excels at what sport?

a. Horseshoes.

b. Darts.

c. Square Dancing.

d. Penuckle.

40. After much experimentation, Jessica finally accepts which Tru:Blood combination?

a. One part A : Two parts B-.

b. Two parts A+ : One part B-.

c. One part 0- : Two parts A-.

d. Two parts 0- : One part B+.

2.1 Answers

1. C. 2. B. 3. C. 4. A. 5. D. 6. C. 7. A. 8. C. 9. B. 10. B. 11. A. 12. B. 13. B. 14. B. 15. D. 16. C. 17. B. 18. B. 19. A. 20. D. 21. B. 22. D. 23. B. 24. C. 25. C. 26. A. 27. C. 28. B. 29. A. 30. D. 31. B. 32. D. 33. C. 34. D. 35. D. 36. A. 37. D. 38. B. 39. C. 40. D.

2.02 KEEP THIS PARTY GOING
Written by: Brian Buckner
Directed by: Michael Lehmann

1. What body part does Eric throw at Lafayette?
a. Foot.
b. Leg.
c. Arm.
d. Head.

2. Why is Eric concerned about the blood in his hair?
a. He has a date in one hour.
b. It is such a waste.
c. He hates B negative.
d. Pam is going to kill him.

3. Why is Sookie embarrassed after making love to Bill?
a. He called her a slattern.
b. She forgot Jessica was in the house.
c. He mentioned a birthmark on her back.
d. They left the lights on.

4. Which of the following, according to Sookie, makes Jessica a typical teen?
a. No humanity.
b. In the grips of overwhelming transformations.
c. Can't control impulses.
d. All of the above.

5. Why did Eric kill Royce?
a. He took silver to him.
b. He tasted bitter.
c. He insulted Pam.
d. He reeked of garlic.

6. What does Lafayette consider his primary role?
a. Capitalist.
b. Prostitute.
c. Fashionista.
d. Survivor.

7. Lafayette will cooperate with Eric if he has what odds of leaving?
a. An ice cube in the Sahara.
b. A cat on a hot tin roof.
c. A candle in the wind.
d. A Jew at an Al Qaeda pep rally.

8. Lafayette informs Eric of whose involvement in Eddie's disappearance?
a. Jason Stackhouse.
b. Sookie Stackhouse.
c. Bill Compton.
d. Tara Thornton.

9. Who does Jason meet on the bus to the Light of Day Institute?
a. Tara Thornton.
b. Luke McDonald.
c. Steve Newlin.
d. Sarah Newlin.

10. Where was Eggs living when Maryann found him?
a. In a garbage dumpster.
b. On a city park bench.
c. An abandoned apartment building.
d. Under a freeway overpass.

11. According to a television newscast, what is Jessica's father's name?
a. John Hamby.
b. David Hamby.

c. Jordan Hamby.

d. Tyler Hamby.

12. What religious sect is run by Reverend Steve Newlin?

a. Temple of the Sun.

b. Followers of the Sun.

c. Fellowship of the Sun.

d. Fellowship of the Light.

13. Where did Luke McDonald play college football?

a. Texas A & M.

b. University of Texas.

c. University of Oklahoma.

d. Ohio State.

14. What does the ring given out at the Light of Day Institute represent?

a. Faith.

b. Fellowship.

c. Honesty.

d. Loyalty.

15. Who does Tara bring along to her shift at Merlotte's?

a. Eggs.

b. JB.

c. Maryann.

d. Andy.

16. At what sport does Jason excel on his first day at LODI?

a. Baseball.

b. Flag football.

c. Volleyball.

d. Cow tipping.

17. Who does Sookie invite to move in with her?

a. Tara.

b. Bill.

c. Jason.

d. Jessica.

18. According to Maryann, her accent comes from which northeastern area?
a. The Hamptons.
b. Greenwich.
c. Kennebunkport.
d. Cape Cod.

19. Where does Ginger shoot Lafayette?
a. His right leg.
b. His left arm.
c. His chest.
d. His left foot.

20. What song is performed at the LODI concert?
a. "Jesus, Take the Wheel."
b. "Jesus Asked Me Out Today."
c. "Jesus Loves Me."
d. "Jesus Is My Homeboy."

21. Why does Jessica think there is something wrong with her?
a. Men refuse to look at her.
b. Her paper cut heals immediately.
c. She hates the taste of blood.
d. She cries blood tears.

22. Where does Sookie offer to take Jessica?
a. Her house.
b. Merlotte's.
c. Fangtasia.
d. The mall.

23. What does the salesperson offer to model for Bill?
a. A nightie.
b. A miniskirt.
c. Daisy Dukes.
d. A gold thong.

24. In a LODI role playing exercise, what does Jason use as a makeshift stake?
a. A chair leg.

b. A table leg.

c. A flag staff.

d. A tree branch.

25. Arlene claims that Terry is sweating like…

a. Iced tea on a hot day.

b. A hooker in church.

c. A vampire at a sunrise service.

d. An ice water pitcher.

26. Which table does Maryann occupy at Merlotte's?

a. One.

b. Two.

c. Three.

d. Four.

27. How many years has Andy Bellefleur been sober?

a. Seven.

b. Eight.

c. Nine.

d. Ten.

28. Who said, "You want respect from people, start by respecting yourself."?

a. Sam.

b. Sookie.

c. Tara.

d. Lafayette.

29. Andy's dancing has been compared to what?

a. An epileptic on meth.

b. Elvis with a hip replacement.

c. A Pip without Gladys Knight.

d. A wet noodle.

30. What is Godric's title?

a. King of Louisiana.

b. Sheriff of Area 9.

c. Sheriff of Area 10.

d. Miss Congeniality.

31. Where does Eric want to take Sookie?

a. Chicago.

b. Shreveport.

c. New Orleans.

d. Dallas.

32. What color car does Sookie drive?

a. Red.

b. Yellow.

c. Green.

d. White.

33. Who does Jessica see looking out the window?

a. Her mother.

b. Her father.

c. Her sister.

d. Her brother.

34. What does Jessica's mother offer make upon her return?

a. Tea.

b. Coffee.

c. Cocoa.

d. Cookies.

35. Who makes a minor pass at Eggs in Merlotte's?

a. Terry.

b. Tara.

c. JB.

d. Jane.

36. What Biblical character does Jason claim walks on water?

a. Jesus.

b. Moses.

c. Noah.

d. Abraham.

37. What is Luke's personal nickname?

a. The Lukester.

b. The Lukemeister.

c. The Lukenator.

d. Big Luke.

38. Why does Lafayette claim he would make a good vampire?

a. He hasn't been to church since the '80s.

b. He sleeps all day anyway.

c. He's so damn pretty.

d. He's already a person of low moral character.

39. How does Jessica describe her mother?

a. Dumber than a sack of hammers.

b. Dumber than a box of rocks.

c. Mean as a swamp rat.

d. Slippery as a snake.

40. Who invites Bill into the Hamby household?

a. Eve Hamby.

b. Eden Hamby.

c. Ellie Hamby.

d. Emma Hamby.

2.2 Answers

1. C. 2. D. 3. B. 4. D. 5. A. 6. D. 7. D. 8. A. 9. B. 10. D. 11. C. 12. C. 13. A. 14. C. 15. C. 16. B. 17. A. 18. D. 19. A. 20. B. 21. D. 22. A. 23. B. 24. C. 25. D. 26. D. 27. C. 28. A. 29. A. 30. B. 31. D. 32. B. 33. C. 34. A. 35. D. 36. B. 37. C. 38. D. 39. A. 40. B.

2.03 SCRATCHES
Written by: Raelle Tucker
Directed by: Scott Winant

1. How is Bill able to restore order in the Hamby household?
a. He glamors the family.
b. He destroys the house by faking a tornado.
c. He places the bodies in the swamp.
d. He isn't able to restore order.

2. Why is Bill angry with Sookie for taking Jessica to her house?
a. She undermined his authority as her maker.
b. She endangered the family's lives as well as their own.
c. All of their lives could have been shattered.
d. All of the above.

3. Sookie knew Bill didn't want her to help Jessica. Why did she help anyway?
a. She thought Bill was overreacting.
b. Jessica blackmailed her.
c. Jessica overpowered her.
d. It reminded her of her grandmother.

4. How does Bill describe Sookie's behavior on the night in question?
a. Like an irresponsible child.
b. Like a spoiled infant.
c. Like a reckless teenager.
d. Like a petulant toddler.

5. How far are they from Bon Temps when Sookie decides to walk?
a. Nearly ten miles.
b. Nearly fifteen miles.
c. Nearly twenty miles.
d. Nearly twenty-five miles.

6. Why does Bill not follow Sookie immediately?
a. He has to take Jessica home.
b. He wants her to learn a lesson.
c. She said she never wants to see him again.
d. He thinks she will come back when she calms down.

7. How does Sookie describe her attacker?
a. A bull.
b. A man-bull.
c. A bull-human.
d. None of the above.

8. After the attack, Bill attempts to give Sookie his blood. What is the result?
a. Nothing happens.
b. She has a seizure.
c. She passes out.
d. She "dies".

9. After going over the receipts three times, Daphne is still short…
a. $64.08.
b. $65.08.
c. $66.08.
d. $67.08.

10. How much does Maryann spend in a single night at Merlotte's?
a. Nearly $100.
b. Nearly $200.
c. Nearly $300.
d. Nearly $400.

11. Who tends to Sookie's wounds?
a. Dr. Ludwig.
b. Dr. Lansing.

c. Dr. Landers.

d. Dr. Feelgood.

12. The poison in Sookie's system is similar to that of which animal?

a. Rattlesnake.

b. Black widow.

c. Gila monster.

d. Komodo dragon.

13. Why doesn't Pam want to search the woods for Sookie's attacker?

a. She's wearing her favorite pumps.

b. She just had her nails done.

c. She doesn't cater to humans.

d. She's wearing a new dress.

14. Who climbs into bed with Jason in a dream?

a. Pam.

b. Tara.

c. Eric.

d. Eddie.

15. Which vampire(s) attempt to give blood to Sookie after her attack?

a. Bill.

b. Bill and Eric.

c. Bill, Eric and Pam.

d. None of the above.

16. Where does Bill spend the day, while Sookie recovers from the attack?

a. In his hidey-hole under the stairs.

b. Longshadow's coffin.

c. In his hidey-hole at Sookie's house.

d. Underground in the cemetery.

17. Name Maryann's chef/ manservant.

a. Carl.

b. James.

c. Jamison.

d. Claude.

18. How does Maryann busy herself while Tara drinks her morning coffee?
a. Pruning flowers.
b. Making Bloody Marys.
c. Rolling joints.
d. Reading *Good Housekeeping*.

19. What explanation does Maryann give Tara for Sam's distrust of her?
a. They have a history.
b. Sam is an alpha male.
c. Sam is afraid of change.
d. Sam is jealous.

20. Who does Sam ask to mind the bar in his absence?
a. Terry.
b. Lafayette.
c. Bill.
d. Sookie.

21. How does Sarah persuade Jason to share his story during group therapy?
a. She reminds him of his vow of honesty.
b. She offers him her pudding.
c. She tells him that forgiveness comes through confession.
d. She doesn't. He isn't ready.

22. To whom does Terry say, "Remind me never to get stuck in a foxhole with you."?
a. Arlene.
b. Sam.
c. Bill.
d. Lafayette.

23. What did Sarah do when the vampires came out of the coffin?
a. She went to a vampire bar to see what all the fuss was about.
b. She marched for equal rights.
c. She rushed to the church and prayed for guidance.
d. She vowed to always walk in the light.

24. What happened to Sarah's sister Amber?
a. She died when Sarah was nine.

b. She ran away from home when Sarah was nine.

c. She got hooked on v.

d. She married a vampire who tortured her.

25. Why does Jason stay at LODI, even though he isn't a vampire victim?

a. Gran and Amy would be alive if he wasn't hooked on v.

b. He has nowhere else to go.

c. He has never finished anything, and he is tired of being a quitter.

d. Steve Newlin convinces him that he shouldn't give up.

26. Ginger makes Sookie a tube top sandwich. What are the ingredients?

a. Peanut butter and honey.

b. Peanut butter and bananas.

c. Peanut butter and marshmallow fluff.

d. Peanut butter and chocolate syrup.

27. How much weight has Ginger lost since she started working at Fangtasia?

a. 35 pounds.

b. 36 pounds.

c. 37 pounds.

d. 38 pounds.

28. How does Sookie discover that Layafette is in the basement?

a. She accidently goes through the wrong door when looking for Bill.

b. She reads Ginger's thoughts.

c. She hears a moaning from downstairs.

d. Ginger lets it slip that he is the reason she is there during the day.

29. Where do they keep the gun at Fangtasia?

a. Under the cash register.

b. Under the bar.

c. Above the bar.

d. In the cash register.

30. Why is Arlene Fowler late for her shift at Merlotte's?

a. Her daughter pierced her son's nose.

b. Her son wrote a curse word on his forehead.

c. She took her son to the hospital after he swallowed silly putty.

d. Her son was throwing up after eating cat food.

31. What does Jessica do when she wakes to find the house empty?
a. She starts crying again.
b. She calls Eric to come get her.
c. She rummages through Bill's "creepy stuff."
d. She gets dressed up and goes to Merlotte's.

32. Who said, "Nice and understanding looks good on you, Sam."?
a. Sookie Stackhouse.
b. Tara Thornton.
c. Maryann Forester.
d. Arlene Fowler.

33. According to Hoyt, Merlotte's chicken fried steak is like a chicken and a steak…
a. Got together and made a baby.
b. Made sweet love.
c. Were sprinkled with fairy dust.
d. Were squashed together with love.

34. How much money does Eric give Sookie for going to Dallas?
a. $5,000.
b. $10,000.
c. $15,000.
d. $20,000.

35. What does Andy Bellefleur find in Maryann's shed?
a. A dog (Sam).
b. A pig.
c. Miss Janette's heart.
d. Jane Bodehouse's pants.

36. For what culinary delight is Sarah Newlin known?
a. Bread pudding.
b. Banana pudding.
c. Chocolate pudding.
d. Chocolate cake.

37. What does Hoyt's mother keep in his closet?
a. Her church dresses.

b. Her hat collection.

c. A doll collection.

d. His baby clothes.

38. What does Hoyt offer to teach Jessica to play?

a. Wii.

b. Monopoly.

c. Chess.

d. Poker.

39. Where does Lafayette want people to believe he has been?

a. Drinking rum in Jamaica.

b. With a cabana boy in Miami.

c. At Club Med.

d. Dancing in Ibiza.

40. Who interrupts Sam's midnight swim?

a. Tara.

b. Maryann.

c. Daphne.

d. Andy.

2.3 Answers

1. A. 2. D. 3. D. 4. A. 5. C. 6. D. 7. C. 8. B. 9. A. 10. C. 11. A. 12. D. 13. A. 14. D. 15. B. 16. B. 17. A. 18. C. 19. D. 20. A. 21. A. 22. B. 23. B. 24. C. 25. A. 26. D. 27. C. 28. B. 29. A. 30. A. 31. D. 32. D. 33. A. 34. B. 35. B. 36. B. 37. C. 38. A. 39. C. 40. C.

2.04 SHAKE AND FINGER POP
Written by: Alan Ball
Directed by: Michael Lehmann

1. Who masterminds the massacre prank against Jason Stackhouse?
a. Luke.
b. Steve.
c. Sarah.
d. Gabe.

2. Blooper Alert: A button on Jason's shirt mysteriously buttons itself. Which button?
a. Top.
b. Second.
c. Third.
d. Fourth.

3. How does Jason "repay" his prankster?
a. Reporting him to the Newlins.
b. Breaking his nose.
c. Breaking his hand.
d. Turning the other cheek.

4. What does Bill threaten to do if Hoyt doesn't leave?
a. Bite him himself.
b. Allow Jessica to have him.
c. Call the authorities.
d. Throw him out a closed window.

5. What is forbidden in the Compton household?
a. Sex.
b. Watching television.
c. Cursing.
d. Hunting.

6. As a vampire, Bill believes he is meant to be what?
a. Tormented.
b. Moody.
c. Depressed.
d. Mysterious.

7. Why will life be different for Jessica than it was for Bill?
a. In his day, humans were prey.
b. Tru:Blood is readily available.
c. Vampires were outlaws.
d. All of the above.

8. Why does Daphne love the dark?
a. The creatures of the night come out.
b. One has to focus on senses other than sight.
c. It is mysterious and sexy.
d. There is nothing to focus on but he stars.

9. How does Sam describe Bon Temps?
a. Paradise.
b. Heaven.
c. Comfortable.
d. Cozy.

10. Daphne craves what unusual breakfast food?
a. Grits.
b. Honey biscuits.
c. Sweet potato pancakes.
d. Cinnamon sugar toast.

11. What is Maryann's parting advice to Tara?
a. Never say, "No," to yourself.
b. Love freely and often.

c. Dance like no one's watching.

d. Live every day like your last.

12. Who does Luke believe was the first vampire?

a. Cain.

b. Able.

c. Jesus.

d. Lazarus.

13. Steve Newlin takes Jason on what type of outing?

a. Camping.

b. Hunting.

c. Paintball.

d. Fishing.

14. Sookie gives Tara a childhood photo for her birthday. Who does it feature?

a. Tara.

b. Tara and Sookie.

c. Tara, Sookie and Gran.

d. Tara, Sookie, Gran and Jason.

15. Mike Spencer suggests what animal as the possible killer of Miss Jeannette?

a. Wolf.

b. Panther.

c. Coyote.

d. Fox.

16. What actually killed Miss Jeannette?

a. Strangulation.

b. Stabbing.

c. Blood loss.

d. Heart removal.

17. What animal does Andy discuss with Kenya?

a. Pig.

b. Werewolf.

c. Panther.

d. Dog.

18. Mike leaves Andy, Kenya and Bud to discuss the case so that he can go where?

a. To dinner.

b. To the gym.

c. Dancing.

d. To Merlotte's.

19. Terry can't make jailhouse chili, because he forgot what key ingredient?

a. Onions.

b. Beans.

c. Corn chips.

d. Catsup.

20. Who tells Sookie that Sam is leaving town?

a. Arlene.

b. Tara.

c. Jason.

d. Terry.

21. What is Tara watching on television when Maryann arrives?

a. The running of the bulls.

b. Hollywood Squares.

c. A vampire talk show.

d. A classic horror film.

22. What song is playing as Sarah Newlin prepares BBQ for Jason and Steve?

a. "Trouble."

b. "Louisiana Hot Sauce."

c. "God Bless Texas."

d. "Playing With Fire."

23. Sarah performs what borderline inappropriate gesture for Jason?

a. Tying his bib.

b. Cutting his meat.

c. Placing his napkin in his lap.

d. Wiping his mouth.

24. Jason is invited to join what "spiritual army"?
a. Army of the Sun.
b. Defenders of the Sun.
c. Defenders of the Faith.
d. Soldiers of the Sun.

25. What is Andy drinking when Sam cuts him off?
a. Vodka.
b. Scotch and Coke.
c. Gin and tonic.
d. Beer.

26. To whom does Lettie Mae give Tara's birthday present?
a. Sam.
b. Andy.
c. Sookie.
d. Maryann.

27. How old is Tara?
a. 25.
b. 26.
c. 27.
d. 28.

28. Bill and Sookie travel to Dallas on what carrier?
a. American.
b. Jet Blue.
c. Anubis.
d. Southwest.

29. Upon exiting the plane, Sookie is greeted by a man with a sign reading what?
a. Stackhouse.
b. Stackhouse Party.
c. Compton.
d. Compton Party.

30. How many free drinks is Sookie given on the flight?
a. Two.

b. Five.

c. Ten.

d. Twelve.

31. How late is Sookie's flight?

a. One hour.

b. Two hours.

c. Three hours.

d. Four hours.

32. What is the name of the driver sent to ambush Sookie?

a. Leon.

b. Linus.

c. Larry.

d. Luther.

33. Where do Sookie and Bill stay while in Dallas?

a. Hotel Charlaine.

b. Hotel Carmina.

c. Hotel Carmilla.

d. Hotel Camino.

34. Which Louisiana residents ultimately travel to Dallas?

a. Sookie and Bill.

b. Sookie, Bill and Jessica.

c. Sookie, Bill, Jessica and Eric.

d. Sookie, Bill, Jessica, Eric and Jason.

35. Why does Lafayette allow Eric to enter his home?

a. He needs Eric's blood.

b. Eric glamors him.

c. Eric threatens to kill him if he doesn't.

d. He doesn't let Eric enter his home.

36. How much does a blood substitute cost in the hotel bar?

a. $30.

b. $35.

c. $40.

d. $45.

37. To what does Eric compare Dallas vampires?

a. Savages.

b. Cowboys.

c. Animals.

d. Gunfighters.

38. Which of the following is not the name of an adult movie offered at the hotel?

a. *Intercourse with the Vampire.*

b. *Bloodlust 4.*

c. *His First Fangbanger.*

d. *Co-Ed Chowdown.*

39. What does Jessica order from room service?

a. Male, straight, B+.

b. Male, straight, B-.

c. Male, straight, O-.

d. Male, straight, AB-.

40. Barry the bellboy possesses what unusual trait?

a. He's a werewolf.

b. He's a witch.

c. He's a fairy.

d. He's a telepath.

2.4 Answers

1. A. 2. C. 3. B. 4. D. 5. D. 6. A. 7. D. 8. B. 9. A. 10. C. 11. A. 12. D. 13. C. 14. C. 15. B. 16. D. 17. A. 18. B. 19. C. 20. D. 21. A. 22. B. 23. A. 24. D. 25. B. 26. A. 27. B. 28. C. 29. D. 30. C. 31. B. 32. A. 33. C. 34. D. 35. A. 36. D. 37. B. 38. B. 39. B. 40. D.

2.05 NEVER LET ME GO
Written by: Nancy Oliver
Directed by: John Dahl

1. To reveal her true self to Sam, Daphne shifts into what animal?
a. Cat.
b. Doe.
c. Fox.
d. Dog.

2. Who interrupts Sam and Darlene in the woods?
a. Sookie.
b. Sookie and Bill.
c. Arlene and Terry.
d. Andy.

3. Sookie knows that the man in the hall has been glamored because his mind is full of...
a. Blank space.
b. Fog and disco music.
c. Romance and poetry.
d. Pleasant simplicity.

4. Jessica informs Bill that he will be sorry when she...
a. Leaves for good.
b. Gets an eating disorder.
c. Snaps.
d. Reports him to Eric.

5. About what is Sookie happy the first night at Hotel Carmilla?
a. It is light tight.
b. The room is secure.
c. Bill won't need to leave the bed.
d. All of the above.

6. What does Bill claim is his only desire?
a. To keep Sookie safe.
b. To please Sookie.
c. To get back to Bon Temps.
d. To find Godric.

7. What is Hoyt's ringtone?
a. "Rumpshaker."
b. "When the Saints Go Marchin In."
c. "Baby Got Back."
d. "Ice, Ice, Baby."

8. What comic book does Hoyt read to Jessica?
a. *Underworld*.
b. *Vamp Boy*.
c. *Space War*.
d. *Space Tomb*.

9. How many pushups is Jason forced to do on his first day of boot camp?
a. 20.
b. 30.
c. 40.
d. 50.

10. What does Tara share with Eggs the morning after the party?
a. A necklace.
b. A diary.
c. A photo.
d. A music box.

11. What does Barry offer as proof that the continental breakfast is, in fact, continental?
a. The French toast is French.

b. The Danishes are Danish.

c. The Belgian waffles are Belgian

d. The Canadian bacon is Canadian.

12. Bill confesses that his lack of control over the Dallas situation makes him feel like…

a. A human.

b. A waitress.

c. An underling.

d. A child.

13. What does Arlene drink while Daphne does her morning prep?

a. Coke.

b. Pepsi.

c. Root beer.

d. Dr. Pepper.

14. What does Daphne like to do after a shift?

a. Dance.

b. Sleep.

c. Run.

d. Swim.

15. Sookie suggests to Barry that he can use his telepathy as a source of what?

a. Gossip.

b. Income.

c. Security.

d. Leverage.

16. How did Bill know Sookie had left the room?

a. He sensed it.

b. He woke and she was gone.

c. He dreamed it.

d. He read her mind.

17. Who said, "You're walking in my shoes and it's giving you blisters."?

a. Tara.

b. Sookie.

c. Arlene.

d. Sarah.

18. Why does Sookie believe she is safe from Eric?

a. He needs her.

b. He wants her.

c. He fears her.

d. He owes her.

19. Despite Arlene's protests, Daphne asks Terry to do what for her?

a. Fill the salt shakers.

b. Sort the silverware.

c. Make the coffee.

d. Make the iced tea.

20. What is the occupation of the first person to crack under the pressure of LODI boot camp?

a. An accountant.

b. A bank teller.

c. A librarian.

d. A school teacher.

21. Tara discovers that the house is not Maryann's, but that of a client in…

a. Brazil.

b. Ecuador.

c. Portugal.

d. Peru.

22. According to Gabe, what should a LODI soldier do when chased by a pack of vampires?

a. Find the nearest stake.

b. Take out as many as you can.

c. Call for backup.

d. Run.

23. Who doesn't live at the Stackhouse home at some point during Season Two?

a. Maryann.

b. Tara.

c. Sookie.

d. Jason.

24. Who does Jason help over the fence?

a. Sarah.

b. Luke.

c. Gabe.

d. Steve.

25. Isabel Beaumont does not believe the Fellowship of the Sun abducted Godric. Why?

a. They fear him.

b. They are cretins.

c. It would be poor P.R.

d. They would have left a trail of clues.

26. Who said, "Vampire church annihilated, wonder who did it,"?

a. Sookie.

b. Isabel.

c. Bill.

d. Eric.

27. What metaphor does Isabel use for Stan's plan?

a. It's a fairy tale.

b. It's a gothic novel.

c. It's a telenovela.

d. It's a movie.

28. Sarah Newlin is jealous of the information shared between Steve and whom?

a. Jason.

b. Gabe.

c. Luke.

d. Nan.

29. What does Stan feel was the vampires' greatest mistake?

a. The Great Revelation.

b. Not killing the Fellowship when the had a chance.

c. Allowing Godric to be taken.

d. Accepting help from a human.

30. LODI's "Research and Development" includes all of the following except...

a. Wooden arrows.

b. Silver bullets.

c. Silver daggers.

d. Throwing stars.

31. Who among the following did not verbally abuse Tara while under Maryann's influence?

a. Arlene.

b. Sam.

c. Lafayette.

d. Sookie.

32. What was the location of the first intimate encounter between Jason Stackhouse and Sarah Newlin?

a. Bathtub.

b. Alter of the Fellowship church.

c. Basement of the Fellowship church.

d. Steve Newlin's bed.

33. Given the choice, Stan Davis prefers what era to the present?

a. The Renaissance.

b. The Old West.

c. The Industrial Revolution.

d. The Middle Ages.

34. Who volunteers to infiltrate the Fellowship of the Sun?

a. Eric.

b. Sookie.

c. Stan.

d. Isabel.

35. Prior to being made vampire, Eric was...

a. A pirate.

b. A Confederate soldier.

c. A Viking.

d. A Spartan.

36. Which of the following does Godric not say he will be for Eric

a. Father.

b. Son.

c. Brother.

d. Child.

37. What is Sam's normal temperature?

a. 98-99.

b. 100-101.

c. 102-103.

d. 103-104.

38. What is Maryann reading when Tara returns to Sookie's house?

a. *Living Dead in Dallas.*

b. *Heart Sick.*

c. *City of Ashes.*

d. *Lovers and Players.*

39. What is Eggs reading when Tara returns to Sookie's house?

a. *Living Dead in Dallas.*

b. *Heart Sick.*

c. *City of Ashes.*

d. *Lovers and Players.*

40. Sookie's and Bill's lovemaking is overheard by what unexpected hotel guest?

a. Eric.

b. Steve Newlin.

c. Godric.

d. Lorena.

2.5 Answers

1. B. 2. C. 3. B. 4. B. 5. D. 6. A. 7. B. 8. D. 9. B. 10. C. 11. B. 12. B. 13. A. 14. C. 15. B. 16. C. 17. B. 18. A. 19. D. 20. B. 21. D. 22. D. 23. D. 24. B. 25. B. 26. B. 27. D. 28. B. 29. A. 30. C. 31. D. 32. A. 33. D. 34. B. 35. C. 36. D. 37. B. 38. B. 39. D. 40. D.

2.06 HARD-HEARTED HANNAH
Written by: Brian Buckner
Directed by: Michael Lehmann

1. Who summons Lorena to Dallas?

a. Bill.

b. Eric.

c. Stan.

d. Godric.

2. Who accompanies Isabel Beaumont to Bill's hotel room?

a. Stan.

b. Godric.

c. Nan.

d. Hugo.

3. Why does Eric summon Lorena to Dallas?

a. To help find Godric.

b. To repay a debt.

c. To separate Bill and Sookie.

d. To provide a diversion.

4. How long has it been since Bill and Lorena last saw each other?

a. Forty years.

b. Fifty years.

c. Sixty years.

d. Seventy years.

5. Who makes a cameo as the hotel's pianist?
a. Alan Ball.
b. Nathan Barr.
c. Jace Everett.
d. Dr. John.

6. The hotel scene flashes back to:
a. 1926.
b. 1927.
c. 1928.
d. 1929.

7. In what city?
a. Savannah.
b. Atlanta.
c. Kansas City.
d. Chicago.

8. What song is Bill singing in the flashback?
a. "Hard Hearted Hannah."
b. "Heart and Soul."
c. 'On the Sunny Side of the Street."
d. "Goin' Back to New Orleans."

9. To attract her victims, Lorena adopts what accent?
a. French.
b. Spanish.
c. German.
d. Italian.

10. What pseudonym does Lorena give?
a. Lordes.
b. Fabienne.
c. Faviana.
d. Fabiana.

11. How does Lorena introduce Bill?
a. Guillermo.
b. Guillaume.

c. Georges.

d. Gilles.

12. Daphne and Sam choose which creative location to do bad things?

a. On the bar.

b. Against the dumpster.

c. In the cooler.

d. On the pool table.

13. How does Carl busy himself while Eggs works on the water heater?

a. Replacing towels.

b. Rubbing Maryann's feet.

c. Making mimosas.

d. Painting Maryann's toenails.

14. What is determined to be faulty with Maryann's water heater?

a. The coils.

b. The heating element.

c. The pump.

d. The wiring.

15. Where do Eggs and Tara need to go for the replacement part?

a. Farraday.

b. Shreveport.

c. Lake Charles.

d. Monroe.

16. How far away is their destination?

a. One hour.

b. Two hours.

c. Three hours.

d. Four hours.

17. What is the focal point of the platform Jason and Luke are building?

a. A guillotine.

b. A pillory.

c. A crucifix.

d. A noose.

18. According to Hugo, what is the primary cause of tension in his relationship with Isabella?
a. Her refusal to let him do the talking.
b. Her reluctance to turn him.
c. Interference from the Dallas vampires.
d. Prejudice.

19. What song is playing on the radio as Tara and Eggs drive?
a. "Dead Flowers".
b. "Thriller".
c. "Don't Fear the Reaper".
d. "Monster Mash".

20. Eggs mysteriously knows to turn at what landmark?
a. Old train station.
b. Overturned truck.
c. Abandoned gas station.
d. Converted barn.

21. How long is Maryann kept waiting for her iced tea?
a. 20 minutes.
b. 10 minutes.
c. 5 minutes.
d. An hour.

22. What explanation does Lafayette give for his extended absence?
a. Illness.
b. A family emergency.
c. A gay cruise.
d. A lost weekend.

23. Andy Bellefleur's interrogation of Lafayette triggers a hallucination of whom?
a. Eddie.
b. Eric.
c. Royce.
d. Pam.

24. Who comes to Lafayette's defense?
a. Terry.
b. Tara.
c. Sookie.
d. Sam.

25. Who composes the lyric "The big ole scary Vampire went to the sun a-fry?"
a. Steve.
b. Luke.
c. Sarah.
d. Jason.

26. Luke lists sex with a male vamp as the ultimate sin. Which of the following does he NOT list by way of comparison?
a. Bestiality.
b. Pedophilia.
c. Adultery.
d. Homosexuality.

27. Sarah Newlin reminds Sookie of what tasty treat?
a. Blow-pops.
b. Angel food cake.
c. Vanilla Pudding.
d. Little Debbies.

28. What pseudonym does Hugo Ayers give to the Newlins?
a. Rufus Dobbs.
b. Rufus Dobson.
c. Riley Dodd.
d. Riley Dillon.

29. What pseudonym does Sookie give?
a. Holly Simpson.
b. Holly Golightly.
c. Susie Snowflake.
d. Susie Simpson.

30. What reason do Sookie and Hugo give for their interest in the Fellowship of the Sun?
a. They hate vampires.
b. They want to feel closer to God's holy light.
c. They need a place to get married.
d. They loved Newlin on Dateline.

31. What do Eggs and Tara find when they return to Sookie's house?
a. A homecooked meal.
b. A murder.
c. An orgy.
d. All of the above.

32. Lorena keeps what item as a reminder of her time with Bill?
a. A picture.
b. A music box.
c. A letter.
d. A necklace.

33. How long does it take Eggs to walk to the site of the ritual?
a. 15 minutes.
b. 30 minutes.
c. 45 minutes.
d. An hour.

34. What two animals cross the street in front of Andy's car?
a. Two deer.
b. A deer and a pig.
c. A deer and a dog.
d. A dog and a pig.

35. Who first orders Lafayette to sell V?
a. Pam.
b. Eric.
c. Ginger.
d. Sophie-Anne.

36. What does Steve Newlin tell Sookie is found below the Fellowship church?

a. An Indian burial ground.

b. His father's tomb.

c. The Rose Line.

d. A rock from the Holy Land.

37. Who prevents Bill from helping Sookie?
a. Eric.

b. Stan.

c. Godric.

d. Lorena.

38. In an act of defiance, Jessica:
a. Dumps Tru:Blood down the drain.

b. Orders pay-per-view vampire porn.

c. Charges long distance calls to Hoyt.

d. All of the above.

39. Jessica receives a late-night visit from whom?
a. Sookie.

b. Bill.

c. Hoyt.

d. Pam.

40. What does Sarah state is Steve Newlin's true motivation?
a. He wants to be more famous than Jesus.

b. He wants to start a war.

c. He wants to be on television.

d. He wants to be a martyr.

2.6 Answers

1. B. 2. D. 3. C. 4. D. 5. B. 6. A. 7. D. 8. A. 9. A. 10. C. 11. B. 12. D. 13. B. 14. C. 15. A. 16. B. 17. C. 18. B. 19. A. 20. D. 21. C. 22. C. 23. B. 24. A. 25. D. 26. B. 27. C. 28. B. 29. A. 30. C. 31. C. 32. D. 33. C. 34. D. 35. A. 36. B. 37. D. 38. A. 39. C. 40. B.

2.07 RELEASE ME
Written by: Raelle Tucker
Directed by: Michael Ruscio

1. Maryann's ritual is disrupted by a gunshot from whom?
a. Sam.
b. Terry.
c. Andy.
d. Bud.

2. Sam escapes Maryann's pursuit by shifting into…
a. An eagle.
b. An owl.
c. A hawk.
d. A bat.

3. Terry Bellefleur stops Andy by breaking…
a. His left arm.
b. His right arm.
c. His left leg.
d. His right leg.

4. Hugo Ayres has what phobia?
a. Claustrophobia.
b. Hydrophobia.
c. Agoraphobia.
d. Sanguivoriphobia (fear of vampires).

5. Which of the following is not a board game found in the basement of the Fellowship of the Sun?
a. Jesus Christ: Vampire Exterminator.
b. Silver and Stakes.
c. Send 'Em Back to Hell.
d. Meet the Sun.

6. Flashback: Where and when does Bill finally stand up to Lorena?
a. Atlanta, 1930.
b. Savannah, 1925.
c. Los Angeles, 1935.
d. New Orleans, 1940.

7. Flashback: Lorena returns early from an evening spent where?
a. A party.
b. A premier.
c. A musical.
d. An opera.

8. Flashback: Lorena offers Bill a young girl that smells like...
a. Peaches.
b. Apricots.
c. Honeysuckle.
d. Roses.

9. Flashback: Lorena attempts to stop Bill's escape by throwing what?
a. A lamp.
b. A vase.
c. A chair.
d. A stake.

10. Eric describes the Soldiers of the Sun as scared little boys with
a. Little guns.
b. Bibles and crossbows.
c. Stakes and chains.
d. Sticks and stones.

11. About what is Eric speaking when he says, "They certainly don't keep well."?

a. Humans.

b. Women.

c. Pets.

d. Soldiers.

12. What does Eric claim is his only interest?

a. Self-preservation.

b. Protecting Sookie.

c. Stopping the Fellowship.

d. Finding Godric.

13. Why does Sarah agree not to tell her husband about her affair with Jason?

a. God comes first.

b. It solves nothing.

c. He doesn't deserve to know.

d. Jason comes first.

14. What is Hoyt Fortenberry's secret?

a. He was adopted.

b. He has never kissed a girl.

c. He is a virgin.

d. He has a girlfriend.

15. How old is Hoyt?

a. 25.

b. 26.

c. 27.

d. 28.

16. Why do Hoyt and Jessica decide to just cuddle their first night together in the hotel?

a. It is almost dawn.

b. Bill could return anytime.

c. The want to wait until the time is right.

d. Sookie is in the adjoining room.

17. What does Eric believe is Stan's true motive?

a. To use Sookie to defeat the Fellowship.

b. To have Godric murdered and claim his title.

c. To be king of Texas.

d. To publicly humiliate the Fellowship.

18. To what does Eggs attribute his blackout?

a. Marijuana.

b. Wine.

c. Exhaustion.

d. Maryann's influence.

19. Who does Sookie say would be ashamed of Newlin?

a. God.

b. Jesus.

c. His father.

d. His mother.

20. Who reveals Sookie's real name to Newlin?

a. Jason.

b. Hugo.

c. Sarah.

d. Gabe.

21. What occurs to a vampire who doesn't rest during the daylight?

a. They die.

b. They become disoriented.

c. They bleed.

d. They start to smoke.

22. Who reveals to Bill that Eric wants Sookie for himself?

a. Sookie.

b. Barry.

c. Lorena.

d. Stan.

23. When describing to Bud Dearborn the ritual in which he was injured, Andy mentions all of the following except...

a. Claws.

b. Bull mask.

c. Saucer eyes.

d. A pig.

24. What does Maryann bring home the morning after the ritual?
a. A dead cat.
b. A dead bird.
c. A dead opossum.
d. A dead rabbit.

25. Who does Newlin order to kill Jason Stackhouse?
a. Sarah.
b. Luke.
c. Gabe.
d. Godric.

26. What reason does Daphne give for Maryann's interest in Sam?
a. She wants to settle an old debt.
b. She can't control him.
c. She wants to share her gift with him.
d. She needs him.

27. What is Maryann?
a. A maenad.
b. A fairy.
c. A shifter.
d. A nymph.

28. Who is ultimately proven to be the Dallas traitor?
a. Isabel.
b. Stan.
c. Godric.
d. Hugo.

29. Maryann is the handmaiden to…
a. Zeus.
b. Aphrodite.
c. Dionysus.
d. Hera.

30. According to Daphne, Maryann is like…
a. A pyro in a room full of matches.
b. An alcoholic at happy hour.

c. An overeater at an all-you-can-eat buffet.

d. A shark in a sea of guppies.

31. Hugo tells Sookie that Bill merely sees her as…

a. A plaything.

b. A blood bag.

c. A trophy.

d. A toy.

32. Lafayette tells his client that the V is going faster than…

a. Joints at a Dead concert.

b. Fritters at a fat farm.

c. Pipes at a crack house.

d. Needles at a crack house.

33. Who does Arlene believe she may have date raped?

a. Sam.

b. Rene.

c. Andy.

d. Terry.

34. Andy bursts into Merlotte's looking for whom?

a. Sam.

b. Rene.

c. Bud.

d. Terry.

35. What song is playing when Hoyt and Jessica make love for the first time?

a. "Bleeding Love."

b. "Strange Love."

c. "My Bloody Valentine."

d. "Black Magic Woman."

36. As a romantic gesture, Hoyt lights blood-scented candles, although to him they smell like…

a. Tin cans.

b. Soap.

c. Soup.

d. Urine.

37. After his escape, Jason is tracked down by...
a. Gabe.
b. Luke.
c. Steve.
d. Sarah.

38. Who killed Daphne?
a. Maryan.
b. Sam.
c. Eggs.
d. Tara.

39. Flashback: What is the one thing Bill claims he wants from Lorena?
a. Freedom.
b. Choice.
c. Forgiveness.
d. Peace.

40. Back in the present, who informs Bill that Sookie is in trouble?
a. Barry.
b. Lorena.
c. Eric.
d. Jason.

2.7 Answers

1. C. 2. B. 3. A. 4. A. 5. D. 6. C. 7. C. 8. B. 9. A. 10. B. 11. A. 12. D. 13. A. 14. C. 15. D. 16. A. 17. B. 18. A. 19. B. 20. B. 21. C. 22. C. 23. D. 24. D. 25. C. 26. B. 27. A. 28. D. 29. C. 30. A. 31. C. 32. B. 33. D. 34. D. 35. A. 36. C. 37. D. 38. C. 39. B. 40. A.

2.08 TIMEBOMB
Written by: Alexander Woo
Directed by: John Dahl

1. Who kills Gabe to protect Sookie?

a. Bill.

b. Eric .

c. Godric.

d. Jason.

2. To whom does Godric refer as "my child"?

a. Eric.

b. Stan.

c. Sookie.

d. Hugo.

3. Who shot Jason Stackhouse in the chest (with a paintball gun)?

a. Steve.

b. Sarah.

c. Luke.

d. Andy.

4. Who first informs Jason that Sookie is at the church?

a. Steve.

b. Eric.

c. Luke.

d. Sarah.

5. What is Sookie's first clue that Godric is Eric's maker?

a. Eric is willing to leave his sheriff position for Godric.

b. Eric speaks of his history with Godric.

c. Eric has a lot of love for Godric.

d. She overhears Eric refer to his maker.

6. When Sookie asks Eric if Godric is his maker, he responds…

a. Don't use words you don't understand.

b. You will understand someday.

c. That is none of your business.

d. As a human, you wouldn't understand.

7. What does Sookie scream to warn Eric he is being attacked?

a. "Behind you!"

b. "Stake!"

c. "Three o'clock!"

d. "Guards!"

8. Eric is willing to sacrifice himself in exchange for the release of whom?

a. Godric.

b. Sookie.

c. Godric and Sookie.

d. Godric, Sookie and Hugo.

9. To whom does Steve Newlin refer as an "evil whore of Satan"?

a. Sookie.

b. Sarah.

c. Isabel.

d. Tara.

10. How does Lorena describe Sookie's constant presence in Bill's thoughts?

a. Like a gnat buzzing around your face.

b. Like a dull fangache.

c. Like a constant buzzing in your ear.

d. Like an alarm clock you can't switch off.

11. With what does Bill attack Lorena?

a. Fireplace tongs.

b. A flat screen television.

c. A stake.

d. The coffee table.

12. What does Bill tell Hoyt, upon finding him in bed with Jessica?

a. Drive her back to Bon Temps before the sun comes up.

b. I warned you never to see her again!

c. I am only trying to protect you.

d. You should not have come here.

13. What tarot card represents Tara's future?

a. Lovers.

b. Justice.

c. Death.

d. Wealth.

14. At what time does Eggs arrive at Merlotte's?

a. 1:00am.

b. 11:45pm.

c. Midnight.

d. 12:10am.

15. What one word allows Jason entrance into the lockdown?

a. Honesty.

b. Brotherhood.

c. Fellowship.

d. Sacrifice.

16. What name appears on Sam's caller ID?

a. Sookie.

b. Merlotte's.

c. Tara.

d. Bon Temps Police.

17. Where does Sam find Daphne's body?

a. The dumpster.

b. A booth at Merlotte's.

c. In Andy Bellefleur's car.

d. In the refrigerator.

18. Where does Jason shoot Newlin?
a. The forehead.
b. The leg.
c. The chest.
d. The back.

19. What color paintball does Jason use to shoot Newlin?
a. Red.
b. Black.
c. Green.
d. Blue.

20. Who said, "Destroy them. All of them."?
a. Newlin.
b. Stan.
c. Eric.
d. Luke.

21. Godric claims to be older than which biblical figure?
a. Jesus.
b. Moses.
c. Abraham.
d. Judus.

22. What does Jason throw at Newlin upon exiting the church?
a. His gun.
b. His stake.
c. A ring.
d. A letter from Sarah.

23. Who escorts Bud to arrest Sam?
a. Kenya.
b. Andy.
c. Maryann.
d. Kevin.

24. Who comes to Sam's defense when he becomes a suspect in Daphne's murder?
a. Sookie.

b. Tara.

c. Lafayette.

d. Andy.

25. On what does Tara blame her recent blackouts?

a. Too much wine.

b. Not enough food in her system.

c. A gas leak.

d. Something in the water.

26. What culinary delight does Maryann prepare for Tara and Eggs?

a. Hunter Souffle.

b. Eggs Forester.

c. Coeur d'orange.

d. Forester casserole.

27. What does Jessica call herself, upon discovering she will be an eternal virgin?

a. A freak of nature.

b. An abomination.

c. A deformity of nature.

d. A freak show.

28. When his guilt is revealed, what is Hugo's sentence?

a. He must spend the rest of his days in service to the nest.

b. He is sentenced to death.

c. He is brutally tortured, then released.

d. He is released unharmed.

29. At the jailhouse, why is Jane unable to greet Sam properly?

a. She lost her pants.

b. She is too intoxicated to walk.

c. She wet herself.

d. She is cuffed to the bed.

30. For what charge was Mike been arrested?

a. Assault.

b. Sodomy.

c. Murder.

d. Reckless endangerment.

31. What does Eric arrange for Godric upon their return to the nest?

a. An O- human.

b. AB+ human.

c. An A+ human.

d. An AB- human.

32. In what unusual foreplay do Eggs and Tara engage after dinner?

a. The pour wine all over themselves.

b. They role around in the leftovers.

c. They beat each other repeatedly.

d. They dance naked in the back yard.

33. Which of the following is not a term used by Lorena to describe Sookie?

a. Meal on wheels.

b. Morsel.

c. Plaything.

d. Blood bag.

34. How does Lorena describe the television with which she was attacked?

a. 72" LCD.

b. 52" plasma.

c. 72" plasma.

d. 65" flat screen.

35. With whom does Bill pick a fight over Sookie?

a. Eric.

b. Sam.

c. Jason.

d. JB.

36. How does Godric describe Lorena's torture of Sookie?

a. Like a spider devouring a fly.

b. Like a cat playing with a mouse.

c. Like a lioness on the hunt.

d. Like a child treats a dragonfly.

37. Following the showdown at the church, to whom does Jason offer a formal apology?

a. Steve.

b. Sarah.

c. Bill.

d. Stan.

38. Why does Godric spare Lorena?

a. It is his choice.

b. Bill asks him to spare her.

c. Eric asks him to spare her.

d. Sookie asks him to spare her.

39. Who escorts Lorena from the Dallas nest?

a. Eric.

b. Hugo.

c. Stan.

d. Bill.

40. What Fellowship of the Sun member is revealed to be a suicide bomber at the episode's cliffhanger ending?

a. Jason.

b. Luke.

c. Sarah.

d. Steve.

2.8 Answers

1. C. 2. A. 3. B. 4. D. 5. C. 6. A. 7. B. 8. C. 9. A. 10. D. 11. B. 12. A. 13. B. 14. D. 15. A. 16. B. 17. D. 18. A. 19. C. 20. B. 21. A. 22. C. 23. A. 24. D. 25. C. 26. A. 27. C. 28. D. 29. A. 30. B. 31. D. 32. C. 33. A. 34. B. 35. A. 36. D. 37. C. 38. A. 39. D. 40. B.

2.09 I WILL RISE UP
Written by: Nancy Oliver
Directed by: Scott Winant

1. Why is Bill not in the Dallas nest during the explosion?
a. He is trapped in the hotel with Lorena.
b. He has run an errand for Eric.
c. He is escorting Lorena from the premises.
d. He is seeking external support.

2. What is the last thing that Bill says to Lorena?
a. You are dead to me.
b. Don't make me see you again.
c. Our paths shall never again cross.
d. Our connection is terminated.

3. How did Sookie survive the explosion?
a. She went out to check on Bill.
b. Eric covered her.
c. She read Luke's thoughts and ducked.
d. Godric shielded her.

4. Which vampire did not survive the explosion?
a. Isabel.
b. Godric.
c. Stan.
d. Nan.

5. How many bullets does Sookie suck out of Eric's body?

a. One.

b. Two.

c. Three.

d. Four.

6. What is left of Luke after the blast?

a. His hand.

b. His leg.

c. His arm.

d. His shoe.

7. According to Bill, why is Eric able to trick Sookie into drinking his blood?

a. No human can resist a vampire forever.

b. He wasn't there to protect her.

c. Eric is the most charismatic vampire in Louisiana.

d. Eric has 1000 years of practice in deceit.

8. Which of the following is not a consequence of Sookie drinking Eric's blood?

a. He can sense her moods.

b. She can't resist his commands.

c. He can track where she is.

d. She will be sexually attracted to him.

9. What does Hoyt want to build for Jessica?

a. A tricked out double-wide.

b. A light-tight love shack.

c. A coffin for two.

d. A mansion in the country.

10. What does Hoyt do to keep Jessica company when she retires to her cubby hole?

a. He taps on the wall.

b. He recites poetry.

c. He reads comics to her.

d. He sings to her.

11. Maryann suggests that, during their blackouts, Eggs and Tara rose to a higher state of…
a. Consciousness.
b. Being.
c. Reality.
d. Enlightenment.

12. Which of the following did ancient mystics not do, according to Maryann?
a. Dance through the streets.
b. Run around naked.
c. Love freely.
d. Act like monkeys.

13. Who said, "I only got your word for it I's matin' with a pine tree."?
a. Mike.
b. Jane.
c. Terry.
d. JB.

14. Where does Sookie go when she can't sleep?
a. Down to breakfast.
b. To find Barry.
c. To Eric's room.
d. To Jason's room.

15. Jason believes people only like him for what?
a. His sex abilities.
b. His athletics.
c. His good looks.
d. All of the above.

16. According to Sarah Newlin, the Fellowship is fighting for all of the following except what?
a. Easter eggs.
b. Babies.
c. Daytime.
d. God's green Earth.

17. Steve Newlin recommends that Nan Flannigan read whom?
a. St. Paul.
b. St. John.
c. St. Luke.
d. St. Mark.

18. Who said, "Go find some roadkill 'cause you ain't eating here."?
a. Lafayette.
b. Terry.
c. Arlene.
d. Sam.

19. According to Arlene, her son will eat what?
a. Dog food, if you put catsup on it.
b. Cat food, if you put mayo on it.
c. Dirt, if you put peanut butter on it.
d. A cow pie, if you put cheese on it.

20. In the wake of all the blackouts and memory lapses, who made a pact to look out for each other?
a. Arlene and Lafayette.
b. Arlene and Terry.
c. Lafayette and Terry.
d. Lafayette and Tara.

21. Which of the following is not Maxine Fortenberry's hate list?
a. African Americans.
b. Methodists.
c. Checkered curtains.
d. Jews.

22. What unique ingredient does Maxine put on Hoyt's grilled cheese sandwich?
a. Hot sauce.
b. Potato chips.
c. Banana slices.
d. Bacon.

23. Who gets into a fight with Eggs over Tara's condition?
a. Sam.
b. Sookie.
c. Lettie Mae.
d. Lafayette.

24. When does Terry tell Arlene he last had sex?
a. Two years ago.
b. More than five years ago.
c. Before the war.
d. He can't remember.

25. Who is the third party in Sookie's dream about Eric?
a. Bill.
b. Lorena.
c. Godric.
d. Sam.

26. What is Eric's response to the statement, "There's love in you."?
a. Don't use words you don't understand.
b. Don't use words I don't understand.
c. Only for Sookie.
d. I am incapable of love.

27. Into what animal does Sam shift to escape from his jail cell?
a. A rat.
b. A housefly.
c. A cockroach.
d. A mouse.

28. How long has Bud been on the force?
a. Over 20 years.
b. Over 30 years.
c. Over 40 years.
d. Over 50 years.

29. What does Maxine tell Jessica a human can give Hoyt that she can't?
a. Breakfast.
b. Babies.

c. A pulse.

d. A church wedding.

30. Who helps Lafayette rescue Tara from Maryann?

a. Sam.

b. Andy.

c. Lettie Mae.

d. Sookie.

31. What are Maryann, Eggs and Tara playing when Lafayette arrives?

a. Strip poker.

b. Twister.

c. Quarters.

d. Scrabble.

32. How was the Fellowship of the Sun able to capture Godric?

a. They baited him with a human.

b. They bound him with silver.

c. He went voluntarily.

d. They threatened to harm Eric if he didn't come peacefully.

33. What is Godric's punishment for the tragedy at the nest?

a. He is banished.

b. He is fired.

c. He is tortured.

d. He is sentenced to death.

34. Who does Maryann demand as a sacrifice for the god to come?

a. Sookie.

b. Eric.

c. Sam.

d. Tara.

35. What is the number of Andy Bellefleur's motel room?

a. 9.

b. 10.

c. 11.

d. 12.

36. Who visits Andy at his motel room on the night of the explosion?
a. Terry.
b. Bud.
c. Portia.
d. Sam.

37. Who is with Godric when he dies?
a. Eric.
b. Newlin.
c. Sookie.
d. No one.

38. How does Bill settle his score with Eric?
a. He hits him with a plasma television.
b. He punches him.
c. He bites him.
d. He reports him to the Queen of Louisiana.

39. How does Godric describe his emotions as the sun rises?
a. He is numb.
b. He is anxious.
c. He is full of joy.
d. He is filled with remorse.

40. What are Godric's last words before greeting the sun?
a. "In this, I see God."
b. "I'm ready to face God."
c. "I kneel before the greatness of God."
d. "Today, I will meet God."

2.9 Answers

1. C. 2. A. 3. B. 4. C. 5. B. 6. A. 7. D. 8. B. 9. A. 10. D. 11. A. 12. C. 13. A. 14. D. 15. D. 16. B. 17. A. 18. C. 19. B. 20. A. 21. D. 22. B. 23. D. 24. D. 25. B. 26. C. 27. B. 28. C. 29. B. 30. C. 31. A. 32. C. 33. B. 34. C. 35. C. 36. D. 37. C. 38. B. 39. C. 40. A.

2.10 NEW WORLD IN MY VIEW
Written by: Kate Barnow & Elisabeth R. Finch
Directed by: Adam Davidson

1. About whom is Sookie dreaming on her ride back to Bon Temps?
a. Eric.
b. Sam.
c. Bill.
d. Jason.

2. The return trip to Bon Temps reminds Jason of what event?
a. His first trip to Texas.
b. The trip back from All State.
c. The day of Gran's funeral.
d. The bus trip to LODI.

3. In what are they traveling?
a. Minivan.
b. Bus.
c. Train.
d. Sedan.

4. Upon entering Bon Temps, Sookie and Jason read lewd graffiti on the sign of what organization?
a. Bon Temps City Hall.
b. Bon Temps Cemetery.
c. Bon Temps Sheriff's Office.
d. Bon Temps Fire Department.

5. Sookie and Jason are made further aware that all is not well when they witness a local resident engaged in what unusual activity?

a. Having sex in the street.

b. Eating raw organs.

c. Banging his head on a post.

d. Streaking.

6. Why does Bill not witness the local resident's behavior?

a. He is in a coffin in the back.

b. He stayed in Dallas to tie up loose ends.

c. He is being held by Lorena.

d. He went ahead to check on Jessica.

7. When his initial offering is deemed inferior, what does Carl offer to arrange as an alternative?

a. Freshly slaughtered mutton.

b. Corn-fed Kobe beef.

c. A suckling pig.

d. A human heart.

8. Who said, "No bug eyes here, just a hangover,"?

a. Jason.

b. Terry.

c. Andy.

d. Lafayette.

9. Andy compares Bon Temps' current state with that of which city?

a. New York City.

b. Calcutta.

c. Dallas.

d. Sodom and Gomorra.

10. Sam is convinced to return to Merlotte's after receiving a call from whom?

a. Lafayette.

b. Tara.

c. Terry.

d. Arlene.

11. Who answers the phone at the Sheriff's office?

a. Bud.

b. Kenya.

c. Maryann.

d. No one.

12. What is the only thing that gets Maxine Fortenberry to focus?

a. Playstation.

b. Wii.

c. Xbox.

d. Xbox 360.

13. To what does Hoyt attribute Maxine's frenzied state?

a. Possession.

b. Too much Jerry Springer.

c. New diet pills.

d. Too much caffeine.

14. Where is "Maryann's"?

a. Merlotte's.

b. Bill's home.

c. Sookie's home.

d. Tara's home.

15. Who said, "This here is the war I been training for?"

a. Bill.

b. Jason.

c. Andy.

d. Terry.

16. How does Sam know that he and Andy are not alone at Merlotte's, despite appearances to the contrary?

a. He hears faint chanting.

b. He hears rustling.

c. He can feel it in the air.

d. He can smell other people.

17. Complete the chant: Lo Lo Bromios, Lo Lo Dendrites, Eleutherios, Enorches…

a. Dionysus.

b. Bacchus.

c. Demetrios.

d. Expelliarmus.

18. Who delivers the only gunshot wound to a member of the Merlotte's mob?

a. Terry.

b. Andy.

c. Sam.

d. Jason.

19. Where do Sam and Andy seek refuge from the angry mob at Merlotte's

a. Under the bar.

b. In the dumpster.

c. In Sam's office.

d. In the freezer.

20. Who does Jane call, after finding their name on the wall at Merlotte's

a. Pumpkin.

b. Peanut.

c. Cocoa.

d. Pickles.

21. What does Lafayette recommend for Tara?

a. Ritalin.

b. Propofol.

c. Thorazine and a padded cell.

d. Vicodin and a straight jacket.

22. Who said, "Jesus and I agreed to see other people, but that don't mean we don't still talk from time to time?"

a. Lafayette.

b. Jason.

c. Lettie Mae.

d. Sookie.

23. When she returns to her home, what does Sookie find on the staircase?

a. A dead cat.

b. A childhood photo.

c. Gran's candlesticks.

d. Her clothing.

24. What color is a maenad's blood?

a. Red.

b. Green.

c. Black.

d. Blue.

25. Assuming she told Sam the truth, what was Daphne's last name?

a. Lawson.

b. Landry.

c. Landers.

d. Linden.

26. Who said, "In the land of the blind, the one-eyed man is king,"?

a. Sam.

b. Sookie.

c. Lafayette.

d. Andy.

27. Which of the following did Jason Stackhouse not use to rescue Sam Merlotte?

a. Luger pistol.

b. Chainsaw.

c. Nail gun.

d. Flares.

28. Which member of the Merlotte's mob is seen drinking directly from the tap?

a. Jane.

b. Mike.

c. Terry.

d. Arlene.

29. A female mob member is allowing revelers to lick what condiment from her legs?

a. Catsup.

b. Mustard.

c. Mayonnaise.

d. Louisana hot sauce.

30. Which member of the Merlotte's mob "always did want to know what human flesh tastes like?"

a. Jane.

b. Mike.

c. Terry.

d. Arlene.

31. Who finally breaks Tara out of her trance?

a. Sookie.

b. Sookie and Bill.

c. Sookie, Bill and Lafayette.

d. Sookie, Bill, Lafayette and Lettie Mae.

32. Who portrays "the god who comes" in an effort to free Sam?

a. Sookie.

b. Bill.

c. Jason.

d. Andy.

33. What found objects become the horns of "the god who comes"?

a. Antlers.

b. Steer horns.

c. Dog bones.

d. Tree branches.

34. What does Sam ask of "the god who comes"?

a. "Spare me."

b. "Spite me."

c. "Smite me."

d. "Spank me."

35. Who declares, "Anyone who wants to debrief me can do so right now,"?

a. Jane.

b. Mike.

c. Terry.

d. Arlene.

36. Complete the quote: "Humans are shockingly susceptible to just about every form of...
a. Thought manipulation."
b. Mental stimulation."
c. Subliminal influence."
d. Coercive persuasion."

37. What promise does Sookie make to Bill before he leaves town?
a. To stay away from Eric.
b. To keep an eye on Jessica.
c. To stay away from Merlotte's.
d. To stay away from her house.

38. A mother's love, part 1: Maxine mockingly compares Hoyt to what movie tough guy?
a. Rocky.
b. Rambo.
c. Dirty Harry.
d. Robocop.

39. From whom does Bill seek advice in defeating the maenad?
a. Eric.
b. Sam.
c. Queen Sophie-Anne.
d. Isabel.

40. It is clear that Bill's host has been feeding, due to the appearance of what bloody body part?
a. Hand.
b. Neck.
c. Arm.
d. Foot.

2.10 Answers

1. A. 2. B. 3. A. 4. D. 5. C. 6. A. 7. B. 8. C. 9. A. 10. D. 11. D. 12. B. 13. C. 14. C. 15. B. 16. D. 17. B. 18. A. 19. D. 20. B. 21. C. 22. A. 23. B. 24. C. 25. B. 26. D. 27. A. 28. B. 29. B. 30. B. 31. B. 32. C. 33. D. 34. C. 35. A. 36. A. 37. D. 38. C. 39. C. 40. D.

2.11 FRENZY

Written by: Alan Ball
Directed by: Daniel Minahan

1. What is Sophie-Anne doing when Bill enters her chamber?
a. Feeding.
b. Having sex.
c. Playing Yahtzee.
d. Reading a magazine.

2. How does Maxine initially react to Jessica feeding on her?
a. She curses at her.
b. She orders Hoyt to take her home.
c. She smiles and says she liked it.
d. She tries to bite Jessica back.

3. According to Sophie-Anne, what is Bill's problem?
a. He is a prude.
b. He is a snob.
c. He needs the company of his own kind.
d. He has become weak.

4. Sophie-Anne recommends that Bill feed upon which member of her court?
a. A Russian boy.
b. A Latvian boy.
c. A Romanian girl.
d. A Croatian girl.

5. What, in Sophie-Anne's mind, ruined everything for Vampires?

a. The Industrial Revoltion.

b. The Cold War.

c. The Sexual Revolution.

d. The Renaissance.

6. What explanation does Sophie-Anne give for Marianne's immortality?

a. Her devotion to Bacchus places her above death.

b. Maenads are the precursors to the contemporary Vampire.

c. She thinks she is immortal, so she is.

d. She has been dead for centuries, but is oblivious to the fact.

7. Bill is warned that he should never underestimate the power of...

a. A maenad scorned.

b. Blind faith.

c. Dark magic.

d. Passion.

8. Why is the Maenad's blood toxic to Bill?

a. Her blood is pure.

b. Her blood is holy.

c. Her blood is inhuman.

d. She has Hep D.

9. When did Sophie-Anne last enjoy heterosexual intercourse?

a. The Nixon Administration.

b. The Kennedy Administration.

c. The Truman Administration.

d. The Eisenhower Administration.

10. Lafayette's handcuffs feature what unusual adornment?

a. Purple fur.

b. Pink fur.

c. Blue feathers.

d. Green feathers.

11. Who does Sam find hiding in the trees behind Merlotte's parking lot?

a. Vampire.

b. Lisa and Coby.

c. Andy.

d. Jason.

12. Complete the quote: Sometimes you need to destroy something to save it. That's in The Bible, or...

a. The Constitution.

b. The Gettysburg Address.

c. Shakespeare.

d. Winnie the Pooh.

13. How long does it take Sookie to receive Bill's text?

a. Two hours.

b. Five hours.

c. Seven hours.

d. Four hours.

14. How long has it been since Coby and Lisa last ate?

a. One day.

b. Two days.

c. Three days.

d. Four days.

15. Who convinces Lafayette to turn over his gun?

a. Sookie.

b. Tara.

c. Lettie Mae.

d. Maryann.

16. What panty-clad citizen is seen running across the BTPD lawn?

a. Maxine.

b. Jane.

c. Portia.

d. Everlee.

17. Who square dances with Andy at the police station?

a. Bud.

b. Kevin.

c. Mike.

d. Jane.

18. Sookie subdues Lettie Mae by throwing what at her head?
a. A Bible.
b. A statue.
c. A vase.
d. A shoe.

19. What is the name of Coby and Lisa Fowler's real father?
a. Duane.
b. Doug.
c. David.
d. Denny.

20. How much money does Sam give Ginger to let the children wait inside Fangtasia?
a. $20.
b. $50.
c. $100.
d. $150.

21. Who summoned Maryann to Bon Temps?
a. Tara.
b. Miss Jeanette.
c. Sam.
d. Lettie Mae.

22. What method does Maryann use to regain her power over Tara?
a. She vibrates.
b. She chants.
c. She holds eye contact.
d. She hits her.

23. How did Hoyt's father die?
a. Stopping a burglary.
b. Car accident.
c. Suicide.
d. Killed in Desert Storm.

24. How old was Hoyt when his father was killed?
a. 8.

b. 9.

c. 10.

d. 11.

25. How does Lafayette distract Arlene and Terry long enough for Sookie to get into her house?

a. He throws drugs.

b. He strips.

c. He runs in the other direction.

d. He threatens Arlene with a knife.

26. What is Pam's interest in the defeat of the maenad?

a. Maenads are bad for business.

b. The excitement. It has been 50 years since her last battle.

c. It owes her a pair of shoes.

d. None. She isn't interested in the affairs of lower creatures.

27. Which of the following is not at term used by Eric to describe children?

a. Humans, but miniature.

b. Microhumans.

c. Teacup humans.

d. Tiny humans.

28. How does Eric get to the Queen's residence?

a. He flies.

b. He runs vamp-speed.

c. Via Anubis Air.

d. Via corvette.

29. What is Jane's offering to the God Who Comes?

a. Her severed finger.

b. Her severed hand.

c. Her son Marvin.

d. Her wedding gown.

30. Mike stops screaming only after Sookie agrees to do what?

a. Kiss him.

b. Sleep with him.

c. Sing to him.

d. Spoon with him.

31. Which of the following is not seen lounging poolside at the Queen's residence?

a. The Queen.

b. Bill.

c. Eric.

d. Hadley.

32. Maryann deflects a bullet, killing whom?

a. Eggs.

b. Carl.

c. Everlee.

d. Portia.

33. What is the Queen's game of choice?

a. Life.

b. Yatzee.

c. Monopoly.

d. Bridge.

34. According to the Queen, money, morality, and gods only exist where?

a. In fairy tales.

b. On television.

c. In human minds.

d. In the movies.

35. Who is Hadley?

a. Bill's great-granddaughter.

b. Sooki'se cousin.

c. Eric's protégée.

d. The new waitress at Merlotte's.

36. Who is revealed to be the source of the vampire blood ring?

a. Bill.

b. Lorena.

c. Sophie-Anne.

d. Pam.

37. What happened to Andy Bellefleur's mother?

a. She was killed in a car accident.

b. She joined the circus.

c. She was killed in a flood.

d. She ran off with a racecar driver.

38. Who persuades Sam to help surrender to the maenad?

a. Sookie.

b. Bill.

c. Eric.

d. Andy.

39. With what does Sookie hit Mike?

a. A shoe.

b. A statue.

c. A frying pan.

d. A vase.

40. What do Eggs and Tara make out of Gran's knitting?

a. A wedding veil.

b. A nest.

c. A web.

d. A baby blanket.

2.11 Answers

1. A. 2. C. 3. B. 4. A. 5. A. 6. C. 7. B. 8. C. 9. D. 10. A. 11. B. 12. A. 13. B. 14. B. 15. C 16. D. 17. A. 18. B. 19. A. 20. C. 21. A. 22. D. 23. C. 24. C. 25. A. 26. C. 27. B. 28. A. 29. A. 30. D. 31. C. 32. B. 33. B. 34. C. 35. B. 36. C. 37. D. 38. B. 39. C. 40. B.

2.12 BEYOND HERE LIES NOTHING
Written by: Alexander Woo
Directed by: Michael Cuesta

1. What unusual request does Lafayette make of Sookie as the episode opens?
a. Lick the egg.
b. Take of your clothes.
c. Obey him.
d. Dance.

2. How old is the vampire blood in Lafayette's body?
a. 100 years.
b. 500 years.
c. 1000 years.
d. 1500 years.

3. Who is the Maid of Honor at Maryann's wedding?
a. Sookie.
b. Tara.
c. Lafayette.
d. Jane.

4. What is unique about Maryann's dress?
a. It is covered in blood.
b. It is 1000 years old.
c. It belonged to Adele Stackhouse.
d. It was imported from Greece.

5. Who are "Old, New and Blue?"

a. Sookie, Lafayette and Tara.

b. Tara, Lafayette and Jane.

c. Tara, Jane and Arlene.

d. Lafayette, Tara and Maxine.

6. Jane always liked Sookie, because she gave her extra:

a. Fries.

b. Pickles.

c. Helpings.

d. Onion rings.

7. Maryann describes Sookie's supernatural gift as:

a. A Bacchanalian miracle.

b. Divinity personified.

c. Divine energy.

d. Nature herself.

8. What song does Maxine sing while dancing around the kitchen?

a. "Party Lights".

b. "The Twist".

c. "Twist and Shout".

d. "Hot, Hot, Hot".

9. How does Hoyt know Maxine is trying to escape?

a. A bell over the door.

b. A string tied to his wrist.

c. A string tied to across the doorway.

d. A bell tied to Maxine's ankle.

10. Maxine refers to Hoyt as which cinematic villain?

a. Freddy Kruger.

b. Hannibal Lecter.

c. Norman Bates.

d. Jason.

11. According to Maryann, what is the food of the gods?

a. The human heart.

b. Lovemaking.

c. Wine.

d. Anger.

12. How does the Queen respond to the news of Godric's death.

a. That stinks.

b. That sucks.

c. That bites.

d. That blows.

13. To what score does the Queen play Yahtzee?

a. 50,000.

b. 500,000.

c. 1,000,000.

d. 5,000,000.

14. Jason just loves the smell of what in the morning?

a. Blood.

b. Nail polish.

c. Hair spray.

d. Beer.

15. Who supplies Eric with vampire blood?

a. Lafayette.

b. Sophie-Anne.

c. Eddie.

d. Pam.

16. How long has Sookie's house been in the family?

a. 100 years.

b. 150 years.

c. 180 years.

d. 200 years.

17. Jason becomes bugeyed after being punched by whom?

a. Arlene.

b. Lafayette.

c. Jane.

d. Andy.

18. What kind of egg is passed around at the wedding?
a. Emu.
b. Ostrich.
c. Alligator.
d. Condor.

19. Who lures Sam to the wedding?
a. Bill.
b. Arlene.
c. Sookie.
d. Tara.

20. Who stabs Sam?
a. Tara.
b. Lafayette.
c. Eggs.
d. Carl.

21. Sam is able to evade, and eventually defeat, Maryann by shifting. Which of the following did he not use against his nemesis?
a. A bull.
b. A deer.
c. A fly.
d. An owl.

22. Who saved Sam's life?
a. Bill.
b. Sookie.
c. Eric.
d. Eggs.

23. Who accompanies Jason when he takes Jane to the emergency room?
a. Sookie.
b. Andy.
c. Arlene.
d. Everlee.

24. Complete the quote: You might have your faults, Andy, but at least you…
a. Didn't let Mike Spencer take ya from behind.

b. Got all your fingers.

c. Got your pants on.

d. Ain't all bug-eyed.

25. Who makes a cameo at Merlotte's?

a. Charlaine Harris.

b. Jace Everett.

c. Nathan Barr.

d. Anne Rice.

26. Sam is able to convince his customers that the recent events were the result of a bad batch of:

a. Mountain Dew.

b. Iced tea.

c. Vodka.

d. Abita.

27. Name the two gossiping Merlotte's patrons who share a fear of aliens.

a. Vanessa and Corine.

b. Vanna and Caroline.

c. Vanelle and Corabeth.

d. Vonetta and Coralee.

28. To what does Jane attribute her lost finger?

a. Gator.

b. Mystery attacker.

c. Hungry vampire.

d. Cooking mishap.

29. What color is the dress Sookie receives from Bill?

a. Pink.

b. Dusty rose.

c. Lavendar.

d. Blue.

30. How many people did Eggs kill?

a. One.

b. Two.

c. Three.

d. Four.

31. Before they leave for their respective evening plans, Bill makes Jessica promise to be home by:

a. 4:00am.

b. 4:30am.

c. 5:00am.

d. 5:30am.

32. What is the first name of Sam's adoptive father?

a. Michael.

b. Gabe.

c. Robert.

d. Mitchell.

33. How long has it been since Sam left home?

a. 16 years.

b. 17 years.

c. 18 years.

d. 19 years.

34. Where does Bill take Sookie for dinner?

a. A home-style Southern restaurant.

b. An Italian restaurant.

c. A French restaurant.

d. It is never specified.

35. Where was the last known address of Sam's birth family?

a. McComb, MS.

b. Magnolia, AR.

c. Marshall, TX.

d. Minden, LA.

36. Name Sam's birth parents.

a. Linda and Jimmy Jack.

b. Malinda and Joe Lee.

c. Laura and Joe Don.

d. Lisa and Jim Bob.

37. What is the surname of Sam's birth family?

a. Michaels.

b. Mershon.

c. Marsdon.

d. Mickens.

38. To what song do Bill and Sookie dance before sitting down to dinner?

a. "Beyond Here Lies Nothing".

b. "Whole Lotta Shakin' Goin' On".

c. "Before the Night Is Over".

d. "Dance Back From the Grave".

39. After dinner, Bill presents Sookie with plane tickets to what Vermont city?

a. Barre.

b. Rutland.

c. Montpelier.

d. Burlington.

40. Who shot Eggs?

a. Jason.

b. Andy.

c. Tara.

d. Carl.

2.12

1. B. 2. C. 3. A. 4. C. 5. C. 6. B 7. D. 8. A. 9. B. 10. C. 11. A. 12. D. 13. B. 14. B. 15. B. 16. B. 17. D. 18. B. 19. A. 20. C. 21. B. 22. A. 23. C. 24. C. 25. A. 26. C. 27. D. 28. A. 29. C. 30. B. 31. A. 32. D. 33. D. 34. C. 35. B. 36. B. 37. D. 38. C. 39. D. 40. A.

SEASON THREE
3.1 BAD BLOOD
Written By: Brian Buckner
Directed By: Daniel Minahan

1. Name the restaurant from which Bill was kidnapped.
a. Maison de Paris.
b. La Petite Vache.
c. Les Trois Chats.
d. Ma Petite Fille.

2. Who attempts to comfort Tara immediately following Eggs' death by wrapping her in a jacket?
a. Bud.
b. Andy.
c. Sam.
d. Lafayette.

3. Name the werewolf that cuts Bill as they ride in the backseat following his abduction.
a. James.
b. Coot.
c. Gus.
d. Louie.

4. Which werewolf is portrayed by the sibling of the late Patrick Swayze?
a. James.
b. Coot.
c. Gus.
d. Louie.

5. Who questions Sookie at the restaurant?

a. Bud.

b. Andy.

c. Kenya.

d. Kevin.

6. How long does Sookie estimate she was in the bathroom before discovering Bill's disappearance?

a. 1-2 minutes.

b. 2-3 minutes.

c. 3-4 minutes.

d. 4-5 minutes.

7. Who consoles Andy after Eggs' death?

a. Tara.

b. Sam.

c. Lafayette.

d. Terry.

8. Tara criticizes Arlene for treating the questioning as if it were what?

a. "The People's Court."

b. A beauty pageant.

c. A job interview.

d. "CSI."

9. What does Lafayette steal from the bar as he and Tara leave the questioning?

a. Vodka.

b. Rum.

c. Whiskey.

d. Tequila.

10. What is the occupation of Jessica's victim?

a. Truck driver.

b. Contractor.

c. Road crew.

d. Mechanic.

11. Jessica's last conversation with the trucker is interrupted when who comes to the door?
a. Bill.
b. Franklin.
c. Andy.
d. Sookie.

12. How does Andy sneak into Jason's home following Eggs' death?
a. Through the basement.
b. Through a window.
c. Through the back door.
d. Through an air vent.

13. The gun that shot Eggs was fired from _____ feet away.
a. 10.
b. 15.
c. 20.
d. 25.

14. What is Pam's favorite color?
a. Blue.
b. Pink.
c. Yellow.
d. Lavender.

15. Yvetta hails from what Balkan state?
a. Latvia.
b. Estonia.
c. Lithuania.
d. Russia.

16. Bill was kidnapped at approximately what time?
a. 9:00pm.
b. 10:00pm.
c. 11:00pm.
d. 12:00am.

17. Before leaving Fangtasia, Sookie informs Eric that he owes her:
a. $5000.

b. $10,000.

c. $15,000.

d. $20,000.

18. Lafayette mixes Tara's alcohol with:

a. Klonopin.

b. Ativan.

c. Valium.

d. Xanax.

19. Who does Eric send to find Bill?

a. Bobby Burnham.

b. Pam.

c. Mr. Reuben.

d. Alcide Herveaux.

20. With whom does Pam encourage Eric to make contact?

a. Queen Sophie-Anne.

b. The Authority.

c. Nan Flanagan.

d. The Magister.

21. In Sam's dream, Bill comments that the water in _____ is quite hard.

a. Alabama.

b. Georgia.

c. Mississippi.

d. Arkansas.

22. Who informs Sam that he has a brother?

a. Amy.

b. Allie.

c. Audrey.

d. Annie.

23. The Mickens were evicted from their last residence _____ year(s) earlier.

a. One.

b. Two.

c. Three.

d. Four.

24. Where does Tommy Mickens work?
a. Cabrio Tires.
b. Cornejo Tires.
c. Camello Tires.
d. Canetta Tires.

25. What is Lorena's last name (in the series)?
a. Krasiki.
b. Polskiej
c. Marek.
d. Który.

26. What does Tommy give as his family name?
a. Harding.
b. Hallow.
c. Herbert.
d. Harmon.

27. Name the reverend that witnesses with Lettie Mae and Tara.
a. Rev. Michaels.
b. Rev. Daniels.
c. Rev. White.
d. Rev. Macalister.

28. The Magister states that blood wasted on anything but procreation is:
a. A cardinal sin.
b. Blasphemy.
c. Sacrilege.
d. Desecration.

29. Arlene determines she is pregnant because she smells what in Lafayette's chili?
a. Paprika.
b. Cloves.
c. Cinnamon.
d. Cayenne.

30. Hoyt and Jason pick up co-eds from:
a. UCLA.

b. NYU.

c. U Conn.

d. LSU.

31. To what career do the co-eds aspire?

a. Doctors.

b. Lawyers.

c. Teachers.

d. Veterinarians.

32. What, according to Queen Sophie-Anne, is really the point?

a. Secularism.

b. Moral anarchy.

c. Relativism.

d. Genocide.

33. Queen Sophie-Anne instructs Eric to sell the blood at what price, if necessary?

a. 10% off.

b. 25% off.

c. 50% off.

d. 75% off.

34. How many days does Pam give Lafayette to sell the V?

a. One.

b. Two.

c. Three.

d. Four.

35. Pam believes people dislike her because she wears too much:

a. Lipstick.

b. Hairspray.

c. Rouge.

d. Pink.

36. Jessica compares her "call" from Bill to the time she drank too much:

a. Vodka.

b. Baileys.

c. Kaluha.

d. Purple Passion.

37. Name the elderly woman on whom Bill feeds.

a. Rose.

b. Olivia.

c. Sadie.

d. Grace.

38. Name her son.

a. Stanley.

b. Sidney.

c. Seymore.

d. Samuel.

39. The woman in question doesn't have a phone, because she claims she was forced to choose between it and what?

a. Oxygen.

b. Food.

c. Medicine.

d. Lights.

40. What is the Mickens' street address?

a. 784 River Street.

b. 20237 River Street.

c. 5689 River Street.

d. 10646 River Street.

3.1 Answers

1. A. 2. D. 3. B. 4. C. 5. C. 6. A. 7. D. 8. B. 9. D. 10. A. 11. D. 12. B. 13. C. 14. D. 15. B. 16. C. 17. B. 18. A. 19. C. 20. A. 21. D. 22. C. 23. C. 24. B. 25. A. 26. D. 27. B. 28. B. 29. C. 30. B. 31. D. 32. B. 33. C. 34. A. 35. D. 36. C. 37. B. 38. A. 39. A. 40. D.

3.02 BEAUTIFULLY BROKEN
Written By: Raelle Tucker
Directed By: Scott Winant

1. What color is Russell Edgington's horse?
a. Chestnut.
b. Black.
c. White.
d. Dapple Gray.

2. How many wolves does Bill kill in his escape attempt?
a. One.
b. Two.
c. Three.
d. Four.

3. Bill rips off whose ear in the process?
a. James'.
b. Coot's.
c. Gus'.
d. Louie's.

4. Lafayette accuses Lettie Mae of being oblivious to Tara's suicide attempt, because she was too busy doing what?
a. Praising Jesus.
b. Praising the bottle.
c. Praising the Rev.
d. Praising herself.

5. What did the rune tattooed on Bill's kidnappers signify?

a. Operation Full Moon.

b. Operation Werewolf.

c. Operation Lupine.

d. Operation Shifter.

6. Which of the following is not an image conjured by Pam to prevent killing her victims?

a. Crying children.

b. Soggy diapers.

c. Puke breath.

d. Maggots.

7. What action of Sookie's makes Eric feel disturbingly human?

a. Kissing him.

b. Hugging him.

c. Slapping him.

d. Crying to him.

8. Eric flashes back to _____ Germany, 1945.

a. Oberammergau.

b. Augsburg.

c. Stuttgart.

d. Leipzig.

9. Talbot informs Bill that his bed once belonged to whom?

a. Vlad Tempest.

b. Marquis de Sade.

c. Jack the Ripper.

d. Countess Elizabeth Báthory.

10. The sterling silver doorknob to Bill's room comes from:

a. Portugal.

b. Libya.

c. Morocco.

d. Egypt.

11. Hoyt brings Jessica a gift of what type Tru:Blood?

a. A-.

b. B+.

c. B-.

d. O-.

12. Hoyt says it is in his nature to do whatever who says?

a. Maxine.

b. Jessica.

c. Summer.

d. Jason.

13. At what hour does Sookie return home to find Jason in her house?

a. 2:00am.

b. 3:00am.

c. 4:00am.

d. 5:00am.

14. Which of the following is not a supernatural being about which Jason questions Sookie?

a. Werewolves.

b. Easter Bunny.

c. Santa.

d. Bigfoot.

15. How does Tommy address his father?

a. Joe Lee.

b. Papa.

c. Pappy.

d. Dad.

16. How old is Sam?

a. 33.

b. 34.

c. 35.

d. 36.

17. What size is the motorcycle boot worn by the werewolf stalking Sookie?

a. 10.

b. 11.

c. 12.

d. 13.

18. Andy sarcastically tells Jason the press conference is in honor of his winning:

a. The lottery.

b. Governor of Louisiana.

c. Miss America.

d. A Mr. Clean lookalike contest.

19. From whom does Sookie get a pistol?

a. Sam.

b. Eric.

c. Terry.

d. Jason.

20. How old was Mrs. Mickens when Sam was born?

a. 15.

b. 16.

c. 17.

d. 18.

21. How long was Mr. Mickens in prison?

a. Six years.

b. Eight years.

c. Ten years.

d. Twelve years.

22. What is the year of the Plymouth Fury Tommy is repairing?

a. 1956.

b. 1958.

c. 1960.

d. 1962.

23. Into what dog breed does Tommy shift?

a. Mastiff.

b. Doberman.

c. Rottweiler.

d. Pit bull.

24. What is the going rate for a chain saw from Bon Temps Hardware?
a. $268.22.
b. $269.22.
c. $270.22.
d. $271.22.

25. How much would it cost to rent one for the night?
a. $39.95.
b. $49.95.
c. $59.95.
d. $69.95.

26. How many children does Jessica's trucker victim have?
a. One.
b. Two.
c. Three.
d. Four.

27. Talbot serves Bill and Russell the blood of a donor who ate only _____ for weeks.
a. Nectarines.
b. Blood Oranges.
c. Tangerines.
d. Peaches.

28. Russell offers to make Bill the Sheriff of:
a. Mississippi, Area Two.
b. Mississippi, Area Three.
c. Mississippi, Area Four.
d. Mississippi, Area Five.

29. Who assists Talbot by draining the Thai boy?
a. Charles.
b. Carlo.
c. Carlos.
d. Carl.

30. Andy mocks Jason by referring to him as:
a. The wind beneath his wings.

b. His own personal Jesus.

c. Rambo without the mullet.

d. His knight in shining armor.

31. Name Sookie's father.

a. Corbett Thomas Stackhouse.

b. Corbett James Stackhouse.

c. Corbin Thomas Stackhouse.

d. Corbin James Stackhouse.

32. Name Sookie's mother.

a. Marie Taylor Stackhouse.

b. Marie Turner Stackhouse.

c. Michelle Taylor Stackhouse.

d. Michelle Turner Stackhouse.

33. With what does Talbot infuse his blood bisque?

a. Rose petals.

b. Mint.

c. Jasmine.

d. Saffron.

34. Who does Talbot claim is as mad as a monkey on a trike?

a. Eric.

b. Sophie-Anne.

c. Franklin.

d. Coot.

35. What does Terry list as the number one reason he should be trusted with children?

a. He has never killed anyone by accident.

b. He loves puppies.

c. He is a nurturer.

d. He has taken anger management classes.

36. Name Terry's armadillo.

a. Buster.

b. Felix.

c. Rex.

d. Spike.

37. What type Tru:Blood does Tara serve Franklin at their first meeting?

a. A-.

b. B+.

c. B-.

d. O-.

38. 586 is the police code for what violation?

a. Illegal parking.

b. Wreckless driving.

c. Public intoxication.

d. Jaywalking.

39. In addition to Russell, who else wears riding gear in this episode?

a. Talbot.

b. Lorena.

c. Bill.

d. Sophie-Anne.

40. Jesus is of what Latino heritage?

a. Puerto Rican.

b. Dominican.

c. Mexican.

d. Cuban.

3.2 Answers

1. C. 2. C. 3. D. 4. A. 5. B. 6. C. 7. D. 8. B. 9. D. 10. C. 11. B. 12. A. 13. D. 14. B. 15. A. 16. B. 17. A. 18. C. 19. C. 20. B. 21. D. 22. B. 23. D. 24. A. 25. B. 26. A. 27. C. 28. A. 29. C. 30. A. 31. B. 32. D. 33. A. 34. B. 35. C. 36. B. 37. B. 38. A. 39. B. 40. C.

3.03 IT HURTS ME TOO
Written By: Alexander Woo
Directed By: Michael Lehmann

1. After killing a werewolf in her home, Eric apologizes to Sookie for damaging her:
a. Dress.
b. Sofa.
c. Rug.
d. Drapes.

2. What year does Talbot give for the tapestry with which Russell douses Lorena's flames?
a. 1385.
b. 1387.
c. 1389.
d. 1391.

3. Russell claims that it is like Armegeddon every time someone chips:
a. A desert glass.
b. A plate.
c. A teacup.
d. A tooth.

4. Where does Eric bury the werewolf?
a. Under the porch.
b. In a fresh grave.

c. In the woods behind Sookie's house.
d. On the side of the road.

5. What is the only thing that Sookie could decipher of the werewolf's thoughts?
a. Edgington.
b. Russell.
c. F.U. Crew.
d. Jackson.

6. Which of the following is not on the list Jason uses to describe police work?
a. Marksmanship.
b. Paramilitary training.
c. Tackling people.
d. Driving fast.

7. Prior to Franklin, how many times does Tara claim to have been in a cheap motel?
a. Never.
b. Once.
c. Twice.
d. Too many to count.

8. Pam instructs Yvetta to lie back and think of:
a. Latvia.
b. Estonia.
c. Lithuania.
d. Russia.

9. By what time would Sookie need to leave in order to reach Jackson by sundown?
a. 2:00am.
b. 3:00am.
c. 4:00am.
d. 5:00am.

10. How long does she plan to be gone?
a. 1-2 days.

b. 2-3 days.

c. 3-4 days.

d. 4-5 days.

11. Jason correctly answers 0 out of _____ on his practice test.

a. 22.

b. 23.

c. 24.

d. 25.

12. Which of the following is not on Jason's list of the two types of people?

a. Those who have dreams but do nothing about it.

b. Those who go out and fulfill their dreams.

c. Those who have no dreams.

d. Those who are scared to dream at all.

13. What is Jason certain he will not need to know for the real test?

a. Speed limit.

b. Age of consent.

c. Blood alcohol limit.

d. Penalty for repeat offenders.

14. Arlene is at least how many weeks pregnant?

a. Nine.

b. Eight.

c. Seven.

d. Six.

15. Who tells Tara about Eggs' funeral?

a. Bud.

b. Mike.

c. Kenya.

d. Andy.

16. Tara claims that things are making her so crazy that she wants to eat what?

a. Her own foot.

b. Glass.

c. Wallpaper.

d. Dirt.

17. Name Bill's son.

a. William Thomas.

b. Thomas Charles.

c. Charles Thomas.

d. William Charles.

18. In what year did he die?

a. 1868.

b. 1869.

c. 1870.

d. 1871.

19. Name Bill's daughter.

a. Susan.

b. Suzanne.

c. Sarah.

d. Sally.

20. What time is it in Jason's test dream?

a. 10:05.

b. 11:05.

c. 12:05.

d. 1:05.

21. What is Sookie doing when she meets Alcide for the first time.

a. Washing dishes.

b. Cleaning the rug.

c. Tanning.

d. Laundry.

22. Mickens dreams of having his own restaurant, entitled what?

a. Mickens' Chickens.

b. Mickens' Chicken 'n Beer.

c. Mickens' Chicken Shack.

d. Mickens' Chicken 'n Chitlins.

23. Who finds the body of Jessica's trucker victim?
a. Hoyt.
b. Jason.
c. Lafayette.
d. JB.

24. Which of the following is not missing from the trucker's body?
a. Head.
b. Feet.
c. Hands.
d. Blood.

25. Bud compares the slew of murders to:
a. Crabgrass.
b. Rabbits.
c. The plague.
d. Katrina.

26. How many years has Bud been on the force?
a. 40 years.
b. 41 years.
c. 42 years.
d. 43 years.

27. In what parish is Herveaux Construction based?
a. Caddo.
b. La Salle.
c. Vermilion.
d. Tensas.

28. Werewolves were able to live in Jackson for nearly how many years without human knowledge?
a. 100.
b. 150.
c. 200.
d. 250.

29. Flashback: When he returns home after being made vampire, Bill's wife Caroline tells him to _____ her.

a. Kill.
b. Turn.
c. Leave.
d. Forget.

30. Flashback: According to Lorena, between the vampire world and the human world lies only:
a. Despair.
b. Anguish.
c. Pain.
d. Suffering.

31. Who claims Johnson is his best man?
a. Russell.
b. Eric.
c. Coot.
d. Franklin.

32. What does Talbot offer Coot to drink?
a. Zima.
b. Colt 45.
c. Boone's Farm.
d. Toilet water.

33. How much does Eric charge Lafayette for the corvette?
a. Nothing.
b. $1.
c. $5.
d. $20.

34. How much does Terry estimate he would have if he got a nickel for every time he heard, "It's not you, it's me?"
a. 5 cents.
b. 10 cents.
c. 15 cents.
d. 20 cents.

35. How many shots does Joe Lee order for Tommy and himself?
a. 10.

b. 12.

c. 14.

d. 16.

36. Who brings Jessica the trucker's head?

a. Franklin.

b. Russell.

c. Talbot.

d. Coot.

37. What does Jason do with his deputy application?

a. Tears it up.

b. Wads it up.

c. Burns it.

d. Throws it in the lake.

38. What is the oldest werewolf bar in Mississippi called?

a. CK9.

b. Lou Pines.

c. Tail of the Pup.

d. The Hairball.

39. What drink does Sookie ask the werewolves to buy her?

a. Cosmo.

b. Gin and tonic.

c. Rum and coke.

d. Long Island ice tea.

40. Bill accuses Lorena of depriving him of all of the following except which?

a. Freedom.

b. Love.

c. Home.

d. Humanity.

3.3 Answers

1. C. 2. B. 3. A. 4. B. 5. D. 6. D. 7. B. 8. B. 9. C. 10. B. 11. A. 12. D. 13. C. 14. A. 15. B. 16. C. 17. B. 18. A. 19. C. 20. B. 21. B. 22. D. 23. A. 24. B. 25. A. 26. D. 27. A. 28. C. 29. A. 30. D. 31. C. 32. A. 33. B. 34. C. 35. B. 36. A. 37. C. 38. B. 39. A. 40. B.

3.04 9 CRIMES
Written By: Kate Barnow and Elisabeth R. Finch
Directed By: David Petrarca

1. What is Sookie bandaging at the top of the episode?

a. Alcide's shoulder.

b. Alcide's hand.

c. Alcide's cheek.

d. Alcide's ribcage.

2. How much time has passed since Debbie moved out?

a. Two weeks.

b. A month.

c. Two months.

d. Three months.

3. What behavior, according to Alcide, goes against everything werewolves stand for?

a. Shifting in front of witnesses.

b. Attacking a woman.

c. Working for a vampire.

d. Doing V.

4. Name Alcide's sister.

a. Jeanette.

b. Janice.

c. Janet.

d. Janelle.

5. Where does Alcide's sister work?

a. Beauty parlor.

b. Flower shop.

c. Truck stop.

d. Strip club.

6. In his first phone call since he went missing, Bill informs Sookie that she is no longer of _____ to him.

a. Interest.

b. Relevance.

c. Importance.

d. Concern.

7. After he catches Tommy in his office, Sam chases him with a:

a. Gun.

b. Bat.

c. Knife.

d. Rolling pin.

8. What form does Tommy take to escape?

a. Bird.

b. Dog.

c. Panther.

d. Wolf.

9. What does Tara tell Franklin Sookie wants?

a. Understanding.

b. Love.

c. Normalcy.

d. Quiet.

10. In the same conversation, Tara confides that who never loved her back?

a. Lettie Mae.

b. Sam.

c. Jason.

d. Eggs.

11. When she insists he can't help but love her again, Bill punches Lorena out of the room, breaking a _____ in the hall.

a. Mirror.

b. Frame.

c. Vase.

d. Chair.

12. In Eric's fantasy, Sookie tells him he smells like _____ in winter.

a. Fire.

b. The air.

c. The mountains.

d. The ocean.

13. Where did Eric play as a child?

a. The North Sea.

b. The Baltic Sea.

c. The Norwegian Sea.

d. The Gulf of Bothnia.

14. In absence of a frying pan, Alcide makes breakfast in a:

a. Mixing bowl.

b. Wok.

c. Muffin pan.

d. Crock pot.

15. Who does Sookie's horoscope?

a. Lettie Mae.

b. Lafayette.

c. Alcide.

d. Janice.

16. Name the high school student on the verge of breaking Jason's passing record.

a. Kitch Maynard.

b. Kitch LeBeau.

c. Kitch Dinkins.

d. Kitch Lackey.

17. What is Kitch's nickname?

a. QB Dooby.

b. QB One.

c. The Big QB.

d. The Big Kitch.

18. What gift does Kevin present to Bud at his retirement party?

a. Cowboy hat.

b. Cowboy boots.

c. Silver spurs.

d. Belt buckle.

19. Which of the following is not on Kenya's list of methods for receiving a promotion?

a. Drink like a fish.

b. Hallucinate about farm animals.

c. Live with your mama.

d. Kill a black man.

20. What is the slang term for a V addict?

a. Blood head.

b. Death chaser.

c. Vamp tapper.

d. Vecker.

21. How long did Bill work for Sophie-Anne?

a. 25 years.

b. 35 years.

c. 45 years.

d. 55 years.

22. What was Bill's job title?

a. Surveyor.

b. Enforcer.

c. Procurer.

d. Assessor.

23. What author does Russell quote while praising a good cigar?

a. Kipling.

b. Conrad.

c. Burroughs.

d. Barrie.

24. Sophie-Anne claims she has been attacked by what organization since the Great Revelation?

a. AVA.

b. VRA.

c. The Authority.

d. IRS.

25. To what does Franklin tie Tara during the day?

a. Chair.

b. Dresser.

c. Radiator.

d. Toilet.

26. What does Franklin bring Tara on his return?

a. Daisies.

b. Roses.

c. Lilies.

d. Tulips.

27. Per Merlotte's policy, parties greater than _____ sit at a table, not the bar.

a. One.

b. Two.

c. Three.

d. Four.

28. How old must one be to serve alcohol in Louisiana?

a. 16.

b. 18.

c. 21.

d. 25.

29. Name the bible study acquaintance that recognizes Jessica at Merlotte's.

a. Chuck.

b. Charles.

c. Chip.

d. Chad.

30. Eric tells Calvin he will kill all his:

a. Brother-cousins.

b. Daddy-brothers.

c. Brother-sons.

d. Uncle-daddies.

31. What is the one thing Franklin misses more than sushi?

a. Good wine.

b. Good cheese.

c. Good steak.

d. Good fruit.

32. Whom does Eric tell Pam to call regarding the Magister?

a. The AVL.

b. The Authority.

c. The VRA.

d. The Queen.

33. Sam offers Mickens a place to stay, with the understanding that there be no further stealing or:

a. Fighting.

b. Looting.

c. Drinking.

d. Lying.

34. Talbot refers to Tara as:

a. Short.

b. Skinny.

c. Tough.

d. Manly.

35. At the strip club, Lorena states that she is in the mood for something _____ and not too fatty.

a. Smoky.

b. Nubile.

c. Cherubic.

d. Fresh.

36. How many days does the Magister give Eric to find Bill Compton?

a. One.

b. Two.

c. Three.

d. Four.

37. Alcide refers to Russell as a "preach and _____" dealer.

a. Run.

b. Practice.

c. Dupe.

d. Teach.

38. What is the stage name of the stripper Bill procures?

a. Sage.

b. Cassidy.

c. Destiny.

d. Desiree.

39. What is her real name?

a. Carol Ann.

b. Camilla Ann.

c. Catrina Ann.

d. Caroline Ann.

40. What color do Alcide's eyes turn when he shifts?

a. Red.

b. Blue.

c. Gold.

d. Black.

3.4

1. A. 2. B. 3. D. 4. B. 5. A. 6. D. 7. A. 8. A. 9. D. 10. C. 11. B. 12. D. 13. A. 14. B. 15. D. 16. A. 17. B. 18. B. 19. C. 20. A. 21. B. 22. C. 23. A. 24. D. 25. D. 26. A. 27. B. 28. B. 29. C. 30. A. 31. D. 32. A. 33. C. 34. B. 35. A. 36. B. 37. D. 38. C. 39. B. 40. A.

3.05 TROUBLE
Written By: Nancy Oliver
Directed By: Scott Winant

1. Who refers to Tara as Franklin's "dusky little blood beast?"
a. Russell.
b. Lorena.
c. Coot.
d. Talbot.

2. Russell refuses to pay Franklin cash because he slaughtered a group of:
a. Elderly women.
b. Children.
c. Tourists.
d. Pregnant women.

3. Where did this slaughter occur?
a. Montgomery.
b. Jackson.
c. Biloxi.
d. Tupelo.

4. Bill refers to Lorena as a tiresome:
a. Bore.
b. Cow.
c. Slattern.
d. Ass.

5. Debbie used to play _____ with Alcide's father.
a. Checkers.
b. Darts.
c. Horseshoes.
d. Chess.

6. She likewise helped Alcide's mother plant:
a. Potatoes.
b. Tomatoes.
c. Green beans.
d. Peas.

7. Who presents Russell with the Stackhouse dossier?
a. Franklin.
b. Bill.
c. Eric.
d. Coot.

8. Talbot refers to himself as the royal:
a. Husband.
b. Concubine.
c. Consort.
d. Courtesan.

9. Talbot is certain Bill is not selling V, because he deems him too:
a. Square.
b. Lazy.
c. Boring.
d. Common.

10. Russell refers to the Magister as a(n) _____ toad.
a. Bloated.
b. Overindulgent.
c. Anachronistic.
d. Self-important.

11. Sookie accuses Debbie of having affairs with all of the following, except whom?
a. Roy.

b. Larry.

c. Bobby.

d. Travis.

12. Franklin attempts to impress Tara with his _____ speed.

a. Cleaning.

b. Typing.

c. Running.

d. Texting.

13. What color mulch does Kenya use for all her gardening?

a. Red.

b. Green.

c. Black.

d. Chocolate.

14. Although he anticipated more action, Jason is forced to cover the BTPD phones for:

a. Everlee.

b. Rosie.

c. Kenya.

d. Kevin.

15. While Jason mans the phones, Kenya investigates a case of vandalism at:

a. Merlotte's.

b. The high school.

c. The cemetery.

d. The library.

16. The Mickens family moves in across the street from:

a. Arlene.

b. Jane.

c. Andy.

d. Maxine.

17. Which of the following is not listed in Terry's definition of a normal relationship?

a. Get fat together.

b. Raise kids.

c. Move in together.

d. Get married.

18. Sam gives Joe Lee a job as what?

a. Bus boy.

b. Handyman.

c. Apartment manager.

d. Cook.

19. Who claims that werewolves are all teeth, fight, and sex?

a. Alcide.

b. Coot.

c. Debbie.

d. Russell.

20. Jason claims that if he doesn't get field work, he will blow up like what?

a. An M-80.

b. A Grenade.

c. Napolean Dynamite.

d. A bazooka.

21. Tara is prevented from escaping Russell's by whom?

a. Talbot.

b. Lorena.

c. Coot.

d. Franklin.

22. What is Lafayette's favorite cigar?

a. Ashton Panatella.

b. Adipati Panatella.

c. Santa Damiana Panatella.

d. Schimmelpenninck Panatella.

23. What evidence does Jesus offer that Lafayette's mother is fine?

a. She threw breakfast in his face.

b. She threw lunch in his face.

c. She threw dinner in his face.

d. She threw her bedpan in his face.

24. To what does Jesus invite Lafayette as a potential first date?
a. A bar.
b. A restaurant.
c. A movie.
d. A dance club.

25. At what time does Lafayette's shift at Merlotte's end?
a. 11:00pm.
b. Midnight.
c. 1:00am.
d. 2:00am.

26. Name Alcide's packmaster.
a. Col. Mustard.
b. Col. Klink.
c. Col. Flood.
d. Col. Borden.

27. What task does Andy give Jason to get him out of the office?
a. Mowing the lawn.
b. Washing the car.
c. Fixing the sprinkler.
d. Washing the windows.

28. Who does Tommy describe as appearing to have been bombed by radiation on his way to middle school?
a. Sam.
b. Lafayette.
c. Hoyt.
d. Terry.

29. How does Crystal know that Jason is not a real cop?
a. He doesn't have a badge.
b. He doesn't have a gun.
c. He doesn't have a shirt.
d. All of the above.

30. While on a date at Merlotte's, Summer informs Hoyt that her father is in:
a. AA.

b. Jail.

c. The Army.

d. Heaven.

31. What reason does Franklin give for tying Tara?

a. To keep her close.

b. To keep her honest.

c. To keep her safe.

d. To keep her pure.

32. What name, in addition to Sookie, was circled in the Stackhouse dossier?

a. Jason.

b. Earl.

c. Adele.

d. Michelle.

33. Bill tells Russell his theory is built of air and _____.

a. Imagination.

b. Fantasy.

c. Dreams.

d. Smoke.

34. To whom does Coot say, "You're a little edgy, bat boy."?

a. Franklin.

b. Talbot.

c. Bill.

d. Eric.

35. The "bat boy" in question retaliates by calling Coot a what?

a. Mongrel.

b. Mutt.

c. Lap dog.

d. Puppy.

36. Where do Jason and Crystal share their first kiss?

a. In his truck.

b. In the woods.

c. In the parking lot.

d. By the lake.

37. What is Tara brought when she claims she is hungry?

a. Daisies.

b. Roses.

c. Lilies.

d. Tulips.

38. When Franklin proposes, he suggests they celebrate at:

a. Denny's.

b. Shoney's.

c. Perkins.

d. IHOP.

39. Talbot attempts to impress Eric with _____ vampire erotica from the 16th Century.

a. Russian.

b. Swedish.

c. French.

d. Japanese.

40. It is revealed that Russell's werewolves killed all of Eric's family except whom?

a. His father.

b. His brother.

c. His sister.

d. His mother.

3.5 Answers

1. D. 2. A. 3. C. 4. B. 5. C. 6. B. 7. A. 8. C. 9. A. 10. C. 11. B. 12. D. 13. A. 14. B. 15. B. 16. A. 17. D. 18. B. 19. A. 20. A. 21. C. 22. D. 23. A. 24. C. 25. A. 26. C. 27. B. 28. C. 29. D. 30. A. 31. C. 32. B. 33. A. 34. C. 35. C. 36. D. 37. C. 38. B. 39. D. 40. B.

3.06 I GOT A RIGHT TO SING THE BLUES
Written By: Alan Ball
Directed By: Michael Lehmann

1. Who does Bill attempt to stake at the top of the episode?

a. Talbot.

b. Russell.

c. Lorena.

d. Franklin.

2. What is Talbot's biggest concern in the aftermath of the attempted staking?

a. The house.

b. His clothes.

c. The lack of decorum.

d. The interruption in conversation.

3. Who threatens to wear Sookie's ribcage as a hat?

a. Talbot.

b. Russell.

c. Lorena.

d. Franklin.

4. Who is ordered to kill Bill?

a. Talbot.

b. Eric.

c. Lorena.

d. Franklin.

5. How old is Russell?

a. Almost 1000.

b. Almost 2000.

c. Almost 3000.

d. Almost 4000.

6. In response to a picky customer, Arlene asks her if she thinks she is at:

a. Applebee's.

b. Shoney's

c. Olive Garden.

d. Red Lobster.

7. Whose cut finger causes Jessica to "pop fang"?

a. Lafayette's.

b. Arlene's.

c. Tommy's.

d. Terry's.

8. To whom does Sookie refer as "big hat, no cattle"?

a. Talbot.

b. Russell.

c. Lorena.

d. Eric.

9. In response to Sookie's claim that she is a waitress, Russell sarcastically responds that he is _____ of Romania.

a. Marie.

b. Elisabeth.

c. Carol.

d. Anne.

10. Who babysits Arlene's children during her shift at Merlotte's?

a. Holly.

b. Terry.

c. Everlee.

d. Rosie.

11. Jessica instructs Arlene's customer to leave the money on the table and head to the:

a. Parking lot.

b. Ladies' room.

c. Door.

d. Kitchen.

12. Where was Jesus born?

a. Catamarca.

b. Córdoba.

c. Rosario.

d. Mendoza.

13. Jesus confides to Lafayette that his mother was:

a. A prostitute.

b. Institutionalized.

c. Raped.

d. Imprisoned.

14. Where do Jesus and Lafayette share their first kiss?

a. In Sam's office.

b. Against the pool table.

c. In Lafayette's car.

d. On Lafayette's sofa.

15. Sookie tells Russell her _____ was a telepath.

a. Cousin.

b. Grandfather.

c. Great grandfather.

d. Uncle.

16. Sookie offers the possible solution that she could be a(n):

a. Alien.

b. Monster.

c. Mental patient.

d. Fairy.

17. Sookie remembers the chain wrapping itself around Mack Rattray "like that _____ thing from Alien."

a. Snake.

b. Octopus.

c. Eel.

d. Crab.

18. Franklin is hurt that Tara didn't notice:

a. He got a haircut.

b. He shaved.

c. He took a shower.

d. He bought new clothes.

19. Franklin refers to Tara as a "wicked little _____."

a. Strumpet.

b. Slattern.

c. Minx.

d. Trollop.

20. How long have Talbot and Russell been together?

a. 600 years.

b. 700 years.

c. 800 years.

d. 900 years.

21. What card game does Eric mistakenly believe he and Talbot are playing?

a. Schafkopf.

b. Kaiserspiel.

c. Schnapsen.

d. Karnoffel.

22. What card game are Talbot and Eric actually playing?

a. Schafkopf.

b. Kaiserspiel.

c. Schnapsen.

d. Karnoffel.

23. Name Russell's driver.

a. Thomas.

b. Trevor.

c. Timothy.

d. Taylor.

24. Who describes werewolves as "base, primitive creatures"?
a. Talbot.
b. Russell.
c. Lorena.
d. Eric.

25. Whose dream is it that supes will one day unite against humans?
a. The Magister's.
b. Sophie-Ann's.
c. Russell's.
d. Lorena's.

26. Eric is concerned that Russell doesn't take the _____ exit.
a. I-10.
b. I-12.
c. I-49.
d. I-55.

27. Jesus briefly leaves Lafayette after finding out that:
a. He is a prostitute.
b. He is an atheist.
c. He dates vampires.
d. He is a V dealer.

28. Which scratch-off game does Sophie-Anne play?
a. Deuces Wild.
b. Gold Rush.
c. Diamond Dazzler.
d. Stacks of Cash.

29. While proposing to Sophie-Anne, Russell promises all of the following, except:
a. To never touch her.
b. To settle her debts.
c. To protect her from the IRS.
d. To give her half his estate.

30. Eric threatens to rip off Sophie-Anne's head and:
a. Throw it in the pool.

b. Feed it to her birds.

c. Feed it to the wolves.

d. Play soccer with it.

31. Name Lorena's maker.

a. Izsák.

b. Ignác.

c. Istvan.

d. Imrus.

32. Who accompanies Coot in interrupting Lorena's torture of Bill?

a. Alcide.

b. Debbie.

c. Franklin.

d. Darrell.

33. Coot dedicates his attack to all of the following, except whom?

a. Louis.

b. Gus.

c. Darrell.

d. Jimmy.

34. Sam's mother makes them a breakfast of _____ fried in bacon grease.

a. Corn fritters.

b. Biscuits.

c. Hoe cakes.

d. Grits.

35. Who is being interviewed with Nan Flanagan as Mrs. Mickens makes breakfast?

a. Rep. David Finch.

b. Rep. Gordon Cotts.

c. Rep. Hollis Lilly.

d. Rep. Grady Boats.

36. With what weapon does Tara attack Franklin?

a. Axe.

b. Spear.

c. Mace.

d. Sickle.

37. What color rose bouquet does Jason bring Crystal?

a. Red.

b. Pink.

c. Yellow.

d. White.

38. Tara tells the werewolf guarding her that Sookie is only allowed to eat what?

a. Almonds.

b. Pistachios.

c. Hazelnuts.

d. Chestnuts.

39. What is on Kitch's license plate?

a. KitchQB.

b. QB One.

c. Big QB.

d. BTHS QB.

40. For whom does Sophie-Anne call as she is being taken away?

a. Russell.

b. Bill.

c. Hadley.

d. Andre.

3.6 Answers

1. B. 2. A. 3. C. 4. C. 5. C. 6. D. 7. B. 8. D. 9. A. 10. B. 11. B. 12. A. 13. C. 14. C. 15. B. 16. A. 17. D. 18. B. 19. A. 20. B. 21. B. 22. D. 23. C. 24. D. 25. C. 26. B. 27. D. 28. A. 29. D. 30. A. 31. C. 32. B. 33. B. 34. A. 35. A. 36. C. 37. D. 38. A. 39. B. 40. C.

3.07 HITTING THE GROUND
Written By: Brian Buckner
Directed By: John Dahl

1. Who tells Lorena she wouldn't know love if it hit her in the fangs?
a. Debbie.
b. Coot.
c. Bill.
d. Sookie.

2. Why did Debbie leave Alcide?
a. He wouldn't marry her.
b. He wouldn't get her pregnant.
c. He wouldn't support her addictions.
d. He wouldn't stand up to his father.

3. What does Sookie do to distract Debbie for Tara?
a. Scream.
b. Hit her.
c. Throw a rock at her.
d. Run in the other direction.

4. Who kills Coot?
a. Tara.
b. Sookie.
c. Bill.
d. Alcide.

5. Who helps Sookie carry Bill to the van?
a. Tara.
b. Alcide.
c. Col. Flood.
d. Eric.

6. In what do they carry Bill?
a. A tarp.
b. A rug.
c. A blanket.
d. A sheet.

7. Who refers to Bill as a "vampire burrito"?
a. Tara.
b. Sookie.
c. Debbie.
d. Alcide.

8. What is written on the side of the van?
a. Herveaux and Company.
b. Herveaux and Son.
c. Herveaux Contracting.
d. Herveaux Construction.

9. Hoyt comes out of the shower to find Jason staring at the ceiling and holding:
a. A billy club.
b. A gun.
c. A knife.
d. A saw.

10. Hoyt bets Jason that Crystal's middle name is what?
a. Chandalier.
b. Ball.
c. Meth.
d. Vase.

11. What are the odds that Hoyt wagers?
a. 100-to-1.

b. 1000-to-1.

c. 1,000,000-to-1.

d. 1,000,000,000-to-1.

12. Who does Eric threaten to drain to get information about Sookie?

a. Tara.

b. Hadley.

c. Lafayette.

d. Sam.

13. What does Summer really want Hoyt to taste?

a. Her cookies.

b. Her biscuits.

c. Her muffins.

d. Her buns.

14. What does Summer say she will do while the boys eat?

a. Spruce.

b. Spiff up.

c. Smarten up.

d. Polish up.

15. According to Eric, what is the only vampire another vampire can trust?

a. A dead one.

b. His maker.

c. His progeny.

d. His queen.

16. How many stars does Eric give Hadley's blood?

a. One.

b. Two.

c. Three.

d. Four.

17. To feed Bill, Sookie cuts her arm with:

a. A saw.

b. A knife.

c. A razor.

d. A piece of glass.

18. Tara claims she hasn't breathed for:
a. Three days.
b. Four days.
c. A week.
d. Two weeks.

19. At the hospital, Sookie is given an unsuccessful transfusion of what blood type?
a. AB+
b. B+.
c. AB-.
d. O-.

20. Name the doctor that attends Sookie at the hospital
a. Dr. Sekular.
b. Dr. Sekuritas.
c. Dr. Sekubis.
d. Dr. Sekion.

21. Where is the hospital?
a. Vienna.
b. Ruston.
c. Downsville.
d. Arcadia.

22. Against which breed of dog does Tommy fight in the ring?
a. Pit bull.
b. Doberman.
c. Rottweiler.
d. Mastiff.

23. How many dogs do we see Sam release from their cages?
a. Five.
b. Six.
c. Seven.
d. Eight.

24. Sam compares his own mother to:
a. Lafayette's.

b. Tara's.

c. Terry's.

d. Hoyt's.

25. Sam refers to his father as a scared man in _____ underpants.

a. Tightie whitey.

b. Dirty.

c. Saggy.

d. Filthy.

26. He states that the Mickens make the Merlottes look like:

a. The Dalai Lama.

b. Mother Theresa.

c. Ghandi.

d. Buddha.

27. Who orders the hospital worker to leave Jason alone?

a. Tara.

b. Sookie.

c. Bill.

d. Lafayette.

28. What is Jason's blood type?

a. AB+

b. B+.

c. AB-.

d. O-.

29. Where was Sookie delivered?

a. In the car.

b. On the dining room table.

c. On the living room floor.

d. In the bathtub.

30. In her fantasy, what does Sookie find by the hospital bed?

a. A goblet.

b. A mirror.

c. A tiara.

d. A scepter.

31. How does Sookie wish to pass her time in the fantasy?
a. Flying.
b. Running.
c. Swimming.
d. Dancing.

32. Who does she meet in the fantasy?
a. Claude.
b. Claudia.
c. Claudine.
d. Claudette.

33. How does this individual refer to Bill?
a. The plague.
b. The death.
c. The drought.
d. The dark.

34. How does she cross between worlds?
a. The pond.
b. The clouds.
c. The light.
d. The river.

35. The Magister gifts Pam with silver earrings from:
a. Zales.
b. Cartier.
c. Tiffany & Co.
d. Harry Winston.

36. He asks if he can pierce her:
a. Eyelids.
b. Tongue.
c. Throat.
d. Nipples.

37. The Magister says that rejection of "The Authority" is:
a. A cardinal sin.
b. Blasphemy.

c. Sacrilege.

d. Desecration.

38. Who asks to rush the Magister's torture due to "cold feet"?

a. Russell.

b. Sophie-Anne.

c. Pam.

d. Eric.

39. When was the Magister made vampire?

a. 8th Century.

b. 9th Century.

c. 10th Century.

d. 11th Century.

40. Where was the Magister made vampire?

a. Scandinavian Peninsula.

b. Arabian Peninsula.

c. Malay Peninsula

d. Iberian Peninsula.

3.7 Answers

1. D. 2. B. 3. A. 4. D. 5. B. 6. A. 7. C. 8. C. 9. A. 10. C. 11. C. 12. B. 13. B. 14. A. 15. C. 16. C. 17. A. 18. C. 19. D. 20. A. 21. B. 22. C. 23. A. 24. B. 25. C. 26. A. 27. D. 28. C. 29. B. 30. A. 31. D. 32. C. 33. D. 34. A. 35. C. 36. A. 37. A. 38. B. 39. B. 40. D.

3.08 NIGHT ON THE SUN
Written By: Raelle Tucker
Directed By: Lesli Linka Glatter

1. To what does Jason initially attribute Sookie's silence?

a. Brain damage.

b. Glamour.

c. Coma.

d. Anger.

2. Which of the following is not one of the things Bill says he wants for Sookie?

a. Lie in the sun.

b. Find a good husband.

c. Have children.

d. Grow old.

3. What is the last thing Bill says to Sookie before he leaves?

a. Be safe.

b. My miracle.

c. I won't call on you again.

d. I love you.

4. What pets accompany Sophie-Anne when she moves to Russell's?

a. Lap dogs.

b. Cats.

c. Alligators.

d. Birds.

5. Where does Talbot bury the werewolves?
a. Under the shed.
b. Under the gazebo.
c. Under the porch.
d. Under the poolhouse.

6. Who tells Russell he is acting like a centuries-old child?
a. Franklin.
b. Talbot.
c. Sophie-Anne.
d. Eric.

7. Talbot finds it difficult to remove Franklin's brains from:
a. The guest linens.
b. The wallpaper.
c. The tapestries.
d. The guestroom rug.

8. Eric states that he enjoys a good _____ as much as the next vampire.
a. Throat slashing.
b. Spine removal.
c. Staking.
d. Head ripping.

9. How long does Eric tell Russell he has been searching for him?
a. 500 years.
b. 1000 years.
c. 1500 years.
d. 2000 years.

10. What reason does he give for the search?
a. He seeks asylum from Sophie-Anne.
b. Godric led him.
c. Russell is a true leader.
d. Russell took his family.

11. What does Terry sing to Arlene's unborn child?
a. "Mockingbird."
b. "Rock-a-Bye Baby."

c. "Beautiful Boy."

d. "Hushaby Mountain."

12. How does Jessica react to Bill's return?

a. She slaps him.

b. She hugs him.

c. She kicks him.

d. All of the above.

13. How does Bill react to Jessica?

a. He hugs her.

b. He calls her a slattern.

c. He releases her.

d. He orders her to leave his home.

14. Who stays with Sookie when she returns from the hospital?

a. Tara.

b. Jason.

c. Sam.

d. Alcide.

15. Who reports Bill to the police?

a. Tara.

b. Jason.

c. Sam.

d. Alcide.

16. Which BTPD member determines that it sounds like a case of assault or attempted murder?

a. Kenya.

b. Kevin.

c. Bud.

d. Andy.

17. Into what dog breed does Sam's mother shift?

a. Pit bull.

b. Doberman.

c. Rottweiler.

d. Mastiff.

18. What does his mother tell Sam is the only thing that will really help?
a. Food.
b. Money.
c. Booze.
d. A fresh start.

19. What does Ruby Jean throw at Lafayette as he tries to enter his home?
a. A statue.
b. A vase.
c. A glass.
d. A plate.

20. What, in addition to vampires, does Ruby Jean say is coming for Lafayette?
a. Werewolves.
b. Witches.
c. Demons.
d. Zombies.

21. Tara claims that, when she looked into Bill's eyes, they were cold and crazy, like:
a. A rattlesnake.
b. A coyote.
c. A panther.
d. A shark.

22. Tara tells Alcide to _____ some sense into Sookie.
a. Charm.
b. Flirt.
c. Glamour.
d. Smush.

23. Alcide responds that Sookie is tougher than a one-eared:
a. Mongrel.
b. Polecat.
c. Alley cat.
d. Yard dog.

24. After swimming to Jason, Crystal tells him all she needs is his:
a. Gun.
b. Truck.
c. Bathroom.
d. Company.

25. Crystal agrees to talk to Jason only after she is given a towel and:
a. Whiskey.
b. Vodka.
c. Beer.
d. Tequila.

26. At what age was Crystal promised to Felton?
a. One.
b. Two.
c. Three.
d. Four.

27. Ruby Jean is able to escape because a new nurse left her in:
a. The foyer.
b. The yard.
c. The garden.
d. The gazebo.

28. After she turns over the knife, Jesus invites Ruby Jean to:
a. Go for a walk.
b. Dance.
c. Watch TV.
d. Play hearts.

29. How many pictures of Bill are there in Sookie's scrapbook?
a. None.
b. One.
c. Two.
d. Three.

30. Eric rises during the day to speak to whom?
a. Sookie.
b. Tara.

c. Lafayette.

d. Hadley.

31. Who is the only one able to snap Talbot out of his artifact-breaking tantrum?

a. Russell.

b. Eric.

c. Franklin.

d. Carlos.

32. What weapon does Jason take to Hot Shot?

a. Chainsaw.

b. Shotgun.

c. Baseball bat.

d. Knife.

33. What is Ruby Jean's illness?

a. Autism.

b. Bipolar Disorder.

c. Schizophrenia.

d. Agoraphobia.

34. What is Ruby Jean's nickname for Lafayette?

a. Fay-Fay.

b. Laffy.

c. Lolly.

d. Lala.

35. When Lafayette was _____, Ruby Jean convinced him he could breathe underwater.

a. Four.

b. Five.

c. Six.

d. Seven.

36. What game acts as Eric's and Talbot's foreplay?

a. Chess.

b. Checkers.

c. Backgammon.

d. Old Maid.

37. Jason finds a Hot Shot resident feeding on a:

a. Pig.

b. Dog.

c. Deer.

d. Rabbit.

38. How many wolves accompany Debbie to Sookie's house?

a. One.

b. Two.

c. Three.

d. Four.

39. With what does Russell burn Bill?

a. Silver chain.

b. Silver badge.

c. Silver belt buckle.

d. Silver spurs.

40. Name the werewolf Jessica kills.

a. James.

b. Coot.

c. Gus.

d. Louie.

3.8 Answers

1. A. 2. B. 3. A. 4. D. 5. B. 6. B. 7. A. 8. D. 9. B. 10. C. 11. A. 12. B. 13. C. 14. D. 15. B. 16. D. 17. D. 18. B. 19. A. 20. B. 21. A. 22. B. 23. C. 24. B. 25. A. 26. D. 27. C. 28. C. 29. B. 30. D. 31. B. 32. B. 33. C. 34. D. 35. B. 36. A. 37. C. 38. B. 39. D. 40. C.

3.09 EVERYTHING IS BROKEN
Written By: Alexander Woo
Directed By: Scott Winant

1. Ginger has a home across the river in:
a. Bossier.
b. Belcher.
c. Benton.
d. Bodcau.

2. Who accompanies Nan Flanagan to Fangtasia?
a. The Magister.
b. The Authority.
c. V-Feds.
d. IRS.

3. How many states is the VRA away from ratification?
a. One.
b. Two.
c. Three.
d. Four.

4. Bill neglects to mention the dead werewolf in Sookie's:
a. Living room.
b. Kitchen.
c. Bathroom.
d. Basement.

5. What do Bill and Sookie use to conceal the werewolf in question?
a. A rug.
b. A blanket.
c. A tarp.
d. A quilt.

6. Which of the following is not one of Jesus' typical excuses to lose dates?
a. Got to go to work early.
b. Meeting with my parole officer.
c. Food poisoning.
d. Could you help me clean the lice out of my bed?

7. What do Lafayette and Jesus drink?
a. Bacardi.
b. Tanqueray.
c. Southern Comfort.
d. Jose Cuervo.

8. Where is Jesus' tattoo?
a. Chest.
b. Arm.
c. Hip.
d. Back.

9. What is the tattoo?
a. Cheetah.
b. Panther.
c. Jaguar.
d. Puma.

10. What is Eric's sign?
a. Virgo.
b. Sagittarius.
c. Leo.
d. Pisces.

11. Via webcam, Nan Flanagan questions Eric on behalf of:
a. The AVA.
b. The Authority.

c. The Magister.

d. The Queen.

12. Who calls Sam to complain about the noise at the Mickens' place?

a. Arlene.

b. Everlee.

c. Terry.

d. Maxine.

13. In what year did Eric nearly catch Russell?

a. 1942.

b. 1943.

c. 1944.

d. 1945.

14. Where did Russell's earlier escape from Eric occur?

a. Augsburg.

b. Friedberg.

c. Stadtbergen.

d. Dasing.

15. At the time, the werewolves were in the service of the:

a. Heer.

b. Kriegsmarine.

c. Luftwaffe.

d. Wermacht.

16. According to Eric, Russell wants to _____ humans.

a. Subjugate.

b. Annihilate.

c. Obliterate.

d. Nullify.

17. Where does Nan plan to fly immediately following her interview with Eric?

a. Houston.

b. Portland.

c. Little Rock.

d. Salt Lake City.

18. Crystal tells Jason that Felton was previously a(n):
a. Marine.
b. Rodeo champion.
c. Amateur boxer.
d. Security guard.

19. Where does Jason leave Felton tied to a tree?
a. Washington Rd.
b. Jackson Rd.
c. Jefferson Rd.
d. Lincoln Rd.

20. Who responds to the call about Felton?
a. Kenya.
b. Kevin.
c. Andy.
d. Bud.

21. Andy claims that his ulcer is so large that _____ is coming out of his belly
button.
a. Coffee.
b. Dr. Pepper.
c. Fresca.
d. Milanta.

22. If Andy finds that the V is coming from Hot Shot, Andy will call the FBI,
DEA, ATF, DOT, and:
a. The Navy Seals.
b. Rambo.
c. Blackwater.
d. The Pentagon.

23. Who does Tara run into at a support group for rape survivors?
a. Holly.
b. Arlene.
c. Mrs. Mickens.
d. Hadley.

24. Where does Hadley ask Sookie to meet her?
a. The aquarium.
b. The park.
c. The cemetery.
d. An abandoned building.

25. In what city do Sookie and Hadley meet?
a. Shreveport.
b. Monroe.
c. Bunkie.
d. Reston.

26. Arlene accuses Tommy of stealing the tip left by whom?
a. Daughters of the Confederacy.
b. Daughters of the Glorious Dead.
c. Decedents of the Glorious Dead.
d. Daughters of the American Revolution.

27. To whom does Arlene confide that Terry is not her baby's father?
a. Sam.
b. Lafayette.
c. Holly.
d. Tara.

28. What skill is revealed when Bill crosses into Faery?
a. He can fly.
b. He can walk on water.
c. He can change form.
d. He can disappear.

29. What is Hunter's favorite fish?
a. The blue one.
b. The orange one.
c. The black one.
d. The striped one.

30. How long have Pam and Eric been together?
a. 100 years.
b. 150 years.

c. 200 years.

d. 250 years.

31. Eric tells Pam it is her time to be:

a. Independent.

b. Released.

c. A leader.

d. A maker.

32. Complete the Summer quote: "Can't do much _____ after dark."

a. Scrapbooking.

b. Quilting.

c. Antiquing.

d. Doll making.

33. Who orders the veggie burger with bacon?

a. JB.

b. Jesus.

c. Hoyt.

d. Summer.

34. When she leaves the table, Summer orders Hoyt to guard her:

a. Burger.

b. Coke.

c. Coat.

d. Dolls.

35. Who orders Eric to bring them Russell's fangs?

a. The Magister.

b. Nan.

c. Pam.

d. Sophie-Anne.

36. What type of stake does Jason use to kill Franklin?

a. Coffee stirrer.

b. A tree branch.

c. A pencil.

d. Wooden bullets.

37. Nan describes the Russell situation as a(n) _____ tar baby.
a. Political.
b. Logistical.
c. Inopportune.
d. Bothersome.

38. On what network does Russell publicly kill the anchorman?
a. WBTN.
b. WNLA.
c. TBBN.
d. TNOL.

39. He kills the anchorman in question by ripping out his:
a. Intestines.
b. Heart.
c. Throat.
d. Spine.

40. Name the weathergirl at the station.
a. Nicole.
b. Tiffany.
c. Wendy.
d. Emily.

3.9 Answers

1. A. 2. C. 3. B. 4. A. 5. C. 6. B. 7. D. 8. A. 9. C. 10. A. 11. B. 12. C. 13. D. 14. A. 15. D. 16. A. 17. B. 18. B. 19. C. 20. B. 21. A. 22. C. 23. A. 24. A. 25. B. 26. A. 27. C. 28. B. 29. A. 30. A. 31. D. 32. C. 33. B. 34. D. 35. B. 36. D. 37. A. 38. C. 39. D. 40. B.

3.10 I SMELL A RAT
Written By: Kate Barnow & Elisabeth R. Finch
Directed By: Michael Lehmann

1. How does Sookie describe her newfound fairy status?

a. Awesome.

b. Confusing.

c. Lame.

d. Ridiculous.

2. According to Bill, every supernatural being believes the Fae were wiped out by:

a. Vampires.

b. Famine.

c. Industrialization.

d. Disease.

3. Name Sookie's fairy godmother.

a. Claudia.

b. Claudine.

c. Claudette.

d. Claude.

4. Where do they dispose of Franklin's remains?

a. In the cemetery.

b. Behind Jason's house.

c. Behind Merlotte's.

d. In the woods.

5. Where are Franklin's clothes hidden?
a. Jason's truck.
b. Merlotte's dumpster.
c. Jason's backyard.
d. The woods.

6. What is Pam's full name?
a. Pamela Swynford DeBellefort.
b. Pamela Swynford DeBeaufort.
c. Pamela Swyntyn DeBeaufort.
d. Pamela Swyntyn DeBellefort.

7. After a fight in the bar, Sam disinfects his hands with:
a. Crown Royal.
b. Jim Beam.
c. Jack Daniels.
d. Southern Comfort.

8. Sam flashes back to his earlier "career" as a jewel thief. What year?
a. 2000.
b. 2001.
c. 2002.
d. 2003.

9. According to legend, what effect does fairy blood have on vampires?
a. Sedation.
b. Intoxication.
c. Stimulation.
d. Hallucination.

10. Which of the following does Bill not include in his list of the elements Sookie has brought back to his life?
a. Love.
b. Light.
c. Hope.
d. Gratitude.

11. To whom does Eric will his estate?
a. To Pam.

b. To Pam and Sookie.

c. To Pam, Sookie, and Ginger.

d. None of the above.

12. Who acts as the witness to the signing of the will?

a. Sookie.

b. Ginger.

c. Pam.

d. Yvetta.

13. Who gives Calvin V to help him heal?

a. Jason.

b. Felton.

c. Crystal.

d. Lafayette.

14. Which of the following does Felton not list among Crystal's duties?

a. Be his wife.

b. Lie under him.

c. Bear his children.

d. Continue the bloodline.

15. Who is Jerry McCafferty?

a. The con artist with whom Sam allied himself.

b. The patron Sam fought at the bar.

c. The anchorman killed by Russell.

d. The lawyer that drew up Eric's will.

16. To where does Eric track Bill and Sookie?

a. The Compton home.

b. The Stackhouse home.

c. Jason's house.

d. Tara's house.

17. Bill tells Eric he has put the cause back _____ years.

a. 100.

b. 1000.

c. 2000.

d. 10,000.

18. Why does Sophie-Anne want Sookie?
a. To read the minds of her enemies.
b. To control Bill and Eric.
c. To walk in the sunlight.
d. As a leverage tool.

19. Who helps Jessica clean the bar alone while Arlene watches Steve Newlin on television?
a. Tommy.
b. Terry.
c. Lafayette.
d. Sam.

20. Complete the Arlene quote: "I may be _____, but I ain't _____."
a. Ditzy, dead.
b. Skinny, evil.
c. Ditzy, evil.
d. Skinny, dead.

21. Summer tells Hoyt he is the most _____ person she's ever met.
a. Spiritual.
b. Beautiful.
c. Special.
d. Strong.

22. What is Summer's nickname for Hoyt.
a. Bear.
b. Pookie.
c. Boo.
d. Puppy.

23. Who does Bill instruct to shoot the werewolves between the eyes.
a. Sookie.
b. Jessica.
c. Jason.
d. Lafayette.

24. How does Jesus describe V?
a. Spiritual.

b. Magic.

c. Transcendent.

d. Evil.

25. According to Lafayette, most people use V for:

a. Healing.

b. Stimulation.

c. Escape.

d. Sex.

26. Lafayette refers to Jesus as _____ in a Sunday hat.

a. Satan.

b. Shaman.

c. Evil.

d. Hell.

27. What does Holly give Sam following his bar fight?

a. Black cohosh.

b. Lemon balm.

c. Passionflower.

d. Magnesium.

28. What is the purpose of the remedy in question?

a. Lowers the heart rate.

b. Lowers adrenaline levels.

c. Lowers testosterone.

d. Lowers inflammation.

29. The two rules in Merlotte's are no dancing and what?

a. No underage drinking.

b. No smoking.

c. No draining.

d. No religion.

30. What does Jason believe is the only thing he is good at?

a. Protecting people.

b. Sex.

c. Football.

d. Screwing up.

31. Name Lafayette's great-great-great grandmother.

a. April.

b. May.

c. June.

d. July.

32. Name her daughter.

a. Winnie.

b. Millie.

c. Nonnie.

d. Lollie.

33. Jesus' _____ was a sorcerer.

a. Father.

b. Grandfather.

c. Great grandfather.

d. Great-great grandfather.

34. Flashback: Into what animal does Sam shift to track the people that fleeced him?

a. Bloodhound.

b. Basset hound.

c. Beagle.

d. English shepherd.

35. Who delivered the memorable quote, "Blah, blah, vampire emergency, blah?"

a. Russell.

b. Pam.

c. Sophie-Anne.

d. Hadley.

36. Whose most admirable quality, according to Eric, is a lack of sentiment?

a. Sookie.

b. Russell.

c. Pam.

d. Sophie-Anne.

37. Where is Eric's farm?

a. Innstrand.

b. Opphaug.

c. Døsvika

d. Ørland.

38. Where did Hoyt go to pray about his relationship with Jessica?
a. Cattle Lake.

b. Swine Lake.

c. Hound Lake.

d. Mutton Lake.

39. Name Russell's male prostitute.
a. Teddy.

b. Tony.

c. Tom.

d. Todd.

40. How much does the prostitute charge for being bitten?
a. $50.

b. $100.

c. $500.

d. $1000.

3.10

1. C. 2. A. 3. B. 4. C. 5. A. 6. B. 7. C. 8. D. 9. B. 10. A. 11. A. 12. D. 13. D. 14. A. 15. C. 16. C. 17. B. 18. C. 19. A. 20. B. 21. C. 22. A. 23. C. 24. B. 25. D. 26. B. 27. A. 28. C. 29. D. 30. A. 31. B. 32. A. 33. B. 34. C. 35. B. 36. C. 37. D. 38. A. 39. B. 40. C.

3.11 FRESH BLOOD
Written By: Nancy Oliver
Directed By: Daniel Minahan

1. Who greets Bill at the door of Fangtasia when he comes for Sookie?
a. Eric.
b. Pam.
c. Russell.
d. Ginger.

2. Who refers to Bill as an infatuated tween?
a. Eric.
b. Pam.
c. Russell.
d. Sookie.

3. Bill is able to be restrained through the use of _____ silver.
a. Colloidal.
b. Laurenian.
c. Mercurial.
d. Lebeauvian.

4. Who administers it?
a. Eric.
b. Pam.
c. Russell.
d. Sookie.

5. Where does Pam keep said silver?

a. Cleavage.

b. Purse.

c. Shoe.

d. Pocket.

6. Who rescues Sookie?

a. Tara.

b. Alcide.

c. Ginger.

d. Yvetta.

7. Pam refers to Sookie as a _____ for Russell.

a. Plaything.

b. Sacrifice.

c. Gift.

d. Decoy.

8. What was Yvetta's job in her homeland?

a. Endocrinologist.

b. Cardiologist.

c. Neurologist.

d. Gynecologist.

9. Who refers to Eric as a lump of muscle with a blood grudge?

a. Russell.

b. Bill.

c. Lafayette.

d. Sookie.

10. What is the relationship between Crystal and Felton?

a. Siblings.

b. Half-siblings.

c. Cousins.

d. Second-cousins.

11. Prior to her revelation that she is a werepanther, what did Jason think Crystal's big secret was?

a. Smoking weed.

b. Jaywalking.

c. Stripping.

d. Shoplifting.

12. All of the confusion has left Jason's brain like:

a. Mashed potatoes.

b. Cheez Whiz.

c. Scrambled eggs.

d. Cocoa Puffs.

13. How does Russell refer to the current situation with Eric?

a. A real pisser.

b. A kick in the pants.

c. Like rain on your wedding day.

d. A crap sandwich.

14. What is Eric's ringtone?

a. "Music of the Night."

b. "I Believe I Can Fly."

c. "Ain't We Got Fun."

d. "Memory."

15. On whom does Pam feed following Sookie's escape?

a. Ginger.

b. Alcide.

c. Yvetta.

d. Tara.

16. How does Sam describe the busboy into whom he crashes?

a. Idiot.

b. Imbecile.

c. Moron.

d. Cretin.

17. Sam keeps the special _____ behind the bar.

a. Whiskey.

b. Vodka.

c. Rum.

d. Scotch.

18. Who tells Sam he is polluting their positive energy vibes?
a. Arlene.
b. Terry.
c. Holly.
d. Lafayette.

19. Who attempts to help Sam?
a. Lafayette.
b. Tommy.
c. Jessica.
d. Terry.

20. Why does Kitch's girlfriend want him to quit practicing?
a. To help her bake cookies.
b. To help her try on outfits.
c. To watch Gossip Girl with her.
d. To braid her hair.

21. Maxine describes Hoyt to Summer as willful and:
a. Dumb.
b. Difficult.
c. Naïve.
d. Hardheaded.

22. Summer complains that she can't reach the top shelf without a:
a. Reacher.
b. Grabber.
c. Getter.
d. Snatcher.

23. According to Maxine, Summer is cute as:
a. Kittens.
b. Cows.
c. Monkeys.
d. Pigs.

24. What does Andy offer Tara when she confronts him about Eggs?
a. Fries.
b. Burger.

c. Onion rings.

d. Tater skins.

25. Who is the only patron to remain behind when Sam clears the bar?

a. Tara.

b. Sookie.

c. Jane.

d. Vonetta.

26. What is Sookie's dream profession?

a. Bank manager.

b. Real estate agent.

c. Flight attendant.

d. Hair dresser.

27. Bill, on the other hand, aspires to teach _____ grade.

a. First.

b. Second.

c. Third.

d. Fourth.

28. In her ritual with Arlene, Holly surrounds them with a circle of _____.

a. Pennies.

b. Lilies.

c. Sage.

d. Salt.

29. Why does she create the circle?

a. Protection.

b. Protection and purity.

c. Protection, purity and fertility.

d. None of the above.

30. Arlene claims to have the body of a tired:

a. Housewife.

b. Teenager.

c. Sow.

d. Broodmare.

31. What does Holly prescribe to Arlene?
a. Decreation.
b. Desemination.
c. Decoction.
d. Detoxtion.

32. Which major university is sending a scout to see Kitch?
a. Texas A & M.
b. Oklahoma.
c. LSU.
d. Georgia Tech.

33. Complete the Russell quote: "Soon there will be _____, then there will be me."
a. Chaos.
b. Armageddon.
c. Apocolypse.
d. Anarchy.

34. During the ritual, Arlene fantasizes about:
a. Mowing.
b. Fishing.
c. Hunting.
d. Gardening.

35. Name Crystal's mentally-challenged "double-cousin."
a. Buford.
b. Bucky.
c. Biff.
d. Bo.

36. Sookie insists that her blood doesn't contain:
a. LSD.
b. Powers.
c. Heroin.
d. Sunscreen.

37. Name the doctor that treats Arlene.
a. Boudreau.

b. Robideaux.

c. Thibodeau.

d. Guilbaut.

38. Eric sarcastically claims to love _____ more when she is cold and heartless.

a. Pam.

b. Sookie.

c. Yvetta.

d. Ginger.

39. During the course of the evening, who among the following feed(s) on Sookie?

a. Eric.

b. Eric and Russell.

c. Eric, Russell, and Pam.

d. Eric, Russell, Pam and Bill.

40. When it becomes clear Eric intends to kill Russell through sun-exposure, he instructs him to be:

a. Dignified.

b. Quiet.

c. Brave.

d. A man.

3.11 Answers

1. B. 2. B. 3. A. 4. B. 5. A. 6. D. 7. C. 8. B. 9. A. 10. B. 11. D. 12. C. 13. B. 14. C. 15. C. 16. C. 17. A. 18. C. 19. D. 20. B. 21. A. 22. B. 23. D. 24. C. 25. A. 26. B. 27. C. 28. D. 29. B. 30. B. 31. C. 32. C. 33. D. 34. B. 35. A. 36. D. 37. B. 38. A. 39. B. 40. C.

3.12 EVIL IS GOING ON
Written By: Alan Ball
Directed By: Anthony Hemingway

1. What does Eric use to keep Russell outside?
a. Silver chain.
b. Silver handcuffs.
c. Silver spurs.
d. Silver shackles.

2. What is the first thing that Godric says in Eric's vision?
a. "Forgive him, Eric."
b. "Release him, Eric."
c. "I am here, my child."
d. "You must release your burden, my child."

3. According to Godric, _____ is all.
a. Humility.
b. Forgiveness.
c. Freedom.
d. Love.

4. Complete the quote: "Only _____ follows death."
a. Eternity.
b. Peace.
c. Love.
d. Life.

5. Sookie dreams of a huge _____ in the forest.

a. Chandelier.

b. Streetlamp.

c. Candelabra.

d. Star.

6. Pam insists that Eric is too weak to _____ fang.

a. Break.

b. Pop.

c. Draw.

d. Drop.

7. What does Sam make Tara for breakfast?

a. Bacon and eggs.

b. Sausage and eggs.

c. Hoe cakes.

d. Biscuits and gravy.

8. Sam describes his adoptive mother as a repressed, co-dependent:

a. Doormat.

b. Milksop.

c. Pushover.

d. Weakling.

9. Tara is hesitant to hear Sam's secret, because she has already had too many supernatural _____ in her life.

a. Monsters.

b. Weirdos.

c. Freaks.

d. Mutants.

10. Sookie drags Russell inside the building with the help of (a) silver:

a. Chain.

b. Hook.

c. Handcuffs.

d. Spray.

11. Who expresses a desire to "reboot?"

a. Sookie.

b. Tara.

c. Sam.

d. Lafayette.

12. When the sun plan fails, Pam encourages Eric to kill Russell via:

a. Decapitation.

b. Staking.

c. Silver bullets.

d. Explosives.

13. Who supervises the road crew in Jason's absence?

a. Lafayette.

b. Hoyt.

c. JB.

d. Rene.

14. What is the population of Bon Temps?

a. 2712.

b. 2512.

c. 2412.

d. 2612.

15. Jason tells the DEA agent he cracked the _____ ring in Hot Shot.

a. Crack.

b. Meth.

c. Cocaine.

d. Blood.

16. After leaving Sam's, Tara flashes back to the murders of all of the following, except:

a. Eggs.

b. Miss Jeanette.

c. Maryann.

d. Franklin.

17. Name the guidance counselor at the high school.

a. Mr. Rantrelle.

b. Mr. Rakestraw.

c. Mr. Rinslow.

d. Mr. Ronstew.

18. What does the counselor keep in his desk?

a. Jose Cuervo.

b. Southern Comfort.

c. Malibu.

d. Baileys.

19. Why does Lafayette come in to Merlotte's early?

a. To make stew.

b. To unload the dishwasher.

c. To ask Sam for a favor.

d. He got locked out of the house.

20. What does Sookie read while supervising Russell?

a. *People.*

b. *In Touch.*

c. *Star.*

d. *Us Weekly.*

21. Sookie informs Russell that his word is worth about as much as tits on a:

a. Tarantula.

b. Turtle.

c. Tomcat.

d. Teacup.

22. In addition to his house, and the deaths of Bill and Eric, how much does Russell offer Sookie to release him?

a. $100,000.

b. $1,000,000.

c. $5,000,000.

d. $10,000,000.

23. Which of the following does Russell not use to describe the drinking of Sookie's blood?

a. Heaven.

b. Arcadia.

c. Nirvana.

d. Paradise.

24. Where does Sookie dispose of Talbot?

a. Dumpster.

b. Trash can.

c. Garbage disposal.

d. Fireplace.

25. Who shot Calvin?

a. Gus.

b. Felton.

c. Jim Jack.

d. Grady.

26. In the Mickens' rush to leave, they do all of the following except:

a. Leave the TV on.

b. Leave the air conditioner on.

c. Leave the refrigerator open.

d. Leave the faucet running.

27. Tara returns home to find her mother in bed with Reverand:

a. Jacobs.

b. White.

c. Daniels.

d. Simmons.

28. Which of the following does not appear in Lafayette's visions?

a. Blood.

b. Bulls.

c. Ghosts.

d. Monster heads.

29. Ginger offers to make Sookie a peanut butter and _____ sandwich while they watch Russell.

a. Mayo.

b. Bacon.

c. Butter.

d. Banana.

30. What does Andy Bellefleur hide in his desk as Jason bursts in?

a. Tequila.

b. Blood.

c. Cigarettes.

d. A photo.

31. Jason gives his license plate number to the DEA agent as "Larry, Charlie, _____ 8M2."

a. Willie.

b. Waylon.

c. Wally.

d. Wyclef.

32. What brand does the DEA agent smoke?

a. Marlboro.

b. Winston.

c. Camel.

d. Lucky Strike.

33. How many days did Jesus spend in a sweat lodge when he first learned magic?

a. One.

b. Two.

c. Three.

d. Four.

34. How many years does Eric predict it will take Russell to escape the cement?

a. 100.

b. 150.

c. 500.

d. 1000.

35. How does Russell describe the time span in question?

a. A holiday.

b. A vacation.

c. A nap.

d. A break.

36. Who does Bill call to kill Eric?
a. Bobby.
b. Reuben.
c. Alcide.
d. Chow.

37. Reverand Newlin is the spokesperson for what rifle brand?
a. Vamp Slayer.
b. Vampire Hunter.
c. Vampire Killer.
d. Vampire Slayer.

38. Eric reveals to Sookie Bill's involvement with Sophie-Anne, as well as his deception regarding:
a. The Rattrays.
b. Maryann.
c. Rene.
d. Russell.

39. Why is Tommy unable to obtain a job?
a. He has no experience.
b. He has no practical skills.
c. He can't read.
d. He's only good at fighting.

40. Where does Claudine appear to Sookie as the episode draws to an end?
a. The forest.
b. The lake.
c. The side of the road.
d. The graveyard.

3.12

1. B. 2. A. 3. D. 4. B. 5. A. 6. D. 7. C. 8. A. 9. C. 10. A. 11. B. 12. A. 13. B. 14. A. 15. D. 16. C. 17. B. 18. C. 19. A. 20. C. 21. B. 22. C. 23. A. 24. C. 25. B. 26. A. 27. C. 28. B. 29. C. 30. B. 31. A. 32. D. 33. C. 34. A. 35. C. 36. B. 37. B. 38. A. 39. C. 40. D.

ACKNOWLEDGMENTS

To Jeff and Chloe for their constant love and support. Without you none of this could have happened.

To Stina, för tålmodigt korrekturläsning utkast efter utkast, utan ett enda klagomål.

Finally, to Shannon, Cass, MK, Ryn, and all the other Belles who make me smile on a daily basis.

ABOUT THE AUTHOR

Sheri Anderson began her Broadway career with the musical *Play On!* To date, she has done 13 Broadway productions, two national tours, and numerous regional and off-Broadway shows. Highlights include the Broadway productions of *The Phantom of the Opera*, *Little Me*, and *The Full Monty*. After decades in the entertainment industry, Anderson became a college professor in 2005, creating such courses as Identity and Alienation in the Drama of Alan Ball. Fields of interest include pop culture, musical theatre and postcolonial drama. She has graduate degrees in theatre and English. In her freetime, she has been directly involved in some of the more popular viral campaigns surrounding <u>True Blood</u>, including "<u>True Blood</u> on Twitter" and Facebook character pages. Anderson is a member of Mensa.